Hans Holbein the Younger: 101 Masterpieces

By Maria Tsaneva

First Edition

*****

Hans Holbein the Younger: 101 Masterpieces
*****

Foreword

Hans Holbein the Younger was German painter, draftsman, and designer renowned for the precise rendering of his drawings and the compelling realism of his portraits, particularly those recording the court of King Henry VIII of England. Holbein was one of the greatest portraitists and most exquisite draftsmen of all time. It is the artist's record of the court of King Henry VIII of England, as well as the taste that he virtually imposed upon that court, that was his most remarkable achievement.

Holbein was a member of a family of important artists. His father, Hans Holbein the Elder, and his uncle Sigmund were renowned for their somewhat conservative examples of late Gothic painting in Germany. One of Holbein's brothers, Ambrosius, became a painter as well, but he apparently died about 1519 before reaching maturity as an artist. The Holbein brothers no doubt first studied with their father in Augsburg; they both also began independent work about 1515 in Basle, Switz. It should be noted that this chronology places Holbein firmly in the second generation of 16th-century German artists. Albrecht Durer, Matthias Grunewald, and Lucas Cranach the Elder all were born between 1470 and 1480 and were producing their mature masterpieces by the time Holbein was just beginning his career. Holbein is, in fact, the only truly outstanding German artist of his generation.

Holbein's work in Basle during the decade of 1515-25 was extremely varied, if also sometimes derivative. Trips to northern Italy (c. 1517) and France (1524) certainly affected the development of his religious subjects and portraiture, respectively. Holbein entered the painters' corporation in 1519, married a tanner's widow, and became a burgher of Basle in 1520. By 1521 he was executing important mural decorations in the Great Council Chamber of Basle's town hall. Unfortunately, none of Holbein's many great frescoes executed here and in England and Germany have survived intact. Their beauty must be judged, instead, from his sketches and copies of the frescoes made by later artists.

Holbein was associated early on with the Basle publishers and their humanist circle of acquaintances. There he found portrait commissions such as that of the humanist scholar Bonifacius Amerbach (1519). In this and other early portraits Holbein showed himself a master of the current German portrait idiom, using robust characterization and accessories, strong gaze, and dramatic silhouette. In Basle, Holbein was also active in designing woodcuts for title pages and book illustrations. He increased his reputation as a book illustrator by a series of woodcuts for the German translation of the Bible by Martin Luther. The artist's most famous work in this area, a series of 41 scenes illustrating the medieval allegorical concept of the Dance of Death, was designed by him and cut by another artist as early as about 1523 to 1526 but was not published until 1538. Its scenes display an immaculate sense of order, packing much information about the lifestyles and habits of Death's victims into a very small format. He completed also a series of pen-and-ink sketches for The Praise of Folie by the Dutch scholar Desiderius Erasmus. In portraiture, too, Holbein's minute sense of observation was soon evident. His first major portrait of Desiderius Erasmus (1523; Louvre, Paris) portrays the Dutch humanist scholar as physically withdrawn from the world, sitting at his desk engaged in his voluminous European correspondence; his hands are as sensitively rendered as his carefully controlled profile.

Protestantism, which had been introduced into Basle as early as 1522, grew considerably in strength and importance there during the ensuing four years. By 1526 severe iconoclastic riots and strict censorship of the press swept over the city. In the face of what, for the moment at least, amounted to a freezing of the arts, Holbein left Basle late in 1526, with a letter of introduction from Erasmus, to travel by way of the Netherlands to England. Only about 28 years old he would achieve remarkable success in England. His most impressive works of this time were executed for the statesman and author Sir Thomas More and included a magnificent single portrait of the humanist (1527). In this image, the painter's close observation extends to the tiny stubble of More's beard, the iridescent glow of his velvet sleeves, and the abstract decorative effects of the gold chain that he wears. Holbein also completed a life-size group portrait of More's family; this work is now lost, though its appearance is preserved in copies and in preparatory drawing in the Kunstmuseum, Basel. This painting was the first example in northern European art of a large group portrait in which the figures are not shown kneeling - the effect of which is to suggest the individuality of the sitters rather than impiety.

Before Holbein journeyed to England in 1526, he had apparently designed works that were both pro- and anti-Lutheran in character. On returning to Basle in 1528, he was admitted, after some hesitation, to the new - and now official - faith. It would be difficult to interpret this as a very decisive change, for Holbein's most impressive religious works, like his portraits, are brilliant observations of physical reality but seem never to have been inspired by Christian spirituality. This is evident in both the claustrophobic, rotting body of the Dead Christ in the Tomb (1521) and in the beautifully composed Family of Burgomaster Meyer Adoring the Virgin (1526). In this latter painting Holbein skillfully combined a late medieval German compositional format with precise Flemish realism and a monumental Italian treatment of form. Holbein apparently quite voluntarily gave up almost all religious painting after about 1530.

In Basle, from 1528 to 1532, Holbein continued his important work for the town council. He also painted what is perhaps his only psychologically penetrating portrait, that of his wife and two children (c. 1528). This picture no doubt conveys some of the unhappiness of that abandoned family. In spite of generous offers from Basle, Holbein left his wife and children in that city for a second time, to spend the last 11 years of his life primarily in England.

By 1533 Holbein was already painting court personalities. His portrait of the statesman Thomas Cromwell brought the artist recognition at court, and by 1536 he was established as court painter to Henry VIII of England. It is estimated that during the last 10 years of his life Holbein executed approximately 150 portraits, life-size and miniature, of royalty and nobility alike. These portraits ranged from a magnificent series depicting German merchants who were working in London to a double portrait of the French ambassadors to Henry VIII's court (1533) to portraits of the king himself (1536) and his different wives, Jane Seymour (1536) and Anne of Cleves (Louvre, Paris). In these and other examples, the artist revealed his fascination with plant, animal, and decorative accessories. Holbein's preliminary drawings of his sitters contain detailed notations concerning jewelry and other costume decorations as well. Sometimes such objects point to specific events or concerns in the sitter's life, or act as attributes referring to a sitter's occupation or character. The relation between accessories and face is a charged and stimulating one, avoiding simple correspondence.

In an analogous fashion, Holbein's mature portraits present an intriguing play between surface and depth. The sitter's outlines and position within the frame are carefully calculated, while inscriptions applied on the surface in gold leaf lock the sitter's head into place. Juxtaposed with this finely tuned two-dimensional design are illusionistic miracles of velvet, fur, feathers, needleworks, and leather. Holbein acted not only as a portraitist but also as a fashion designer for the court. The artist made designs for all the state robes of the king; he left, in addition, more than 250 delicate drawings for everything from buttons and buckles to pageant weapons, horse outfittings, and bookbindings for the royal household. This choice of work indicates Holbein's Mannerist concentration on surface texture and detail of design, a concern that in some ways precluded the incorporation of great psychological depth in his portraits. Holbein died in a London plague epidemic in 1543.

Paintings and Drawings

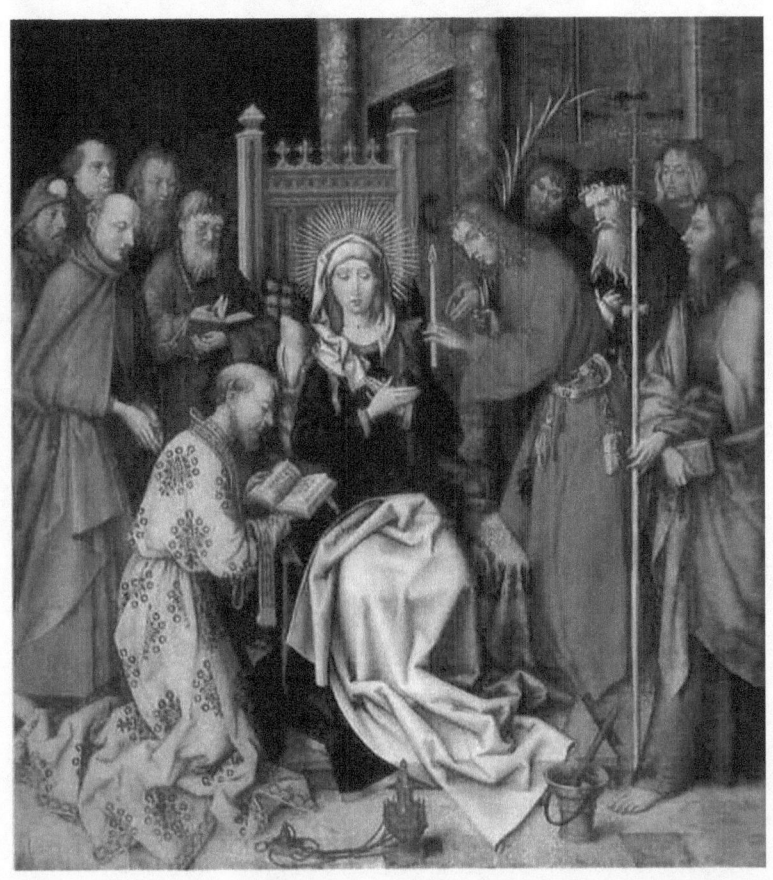

Death of the Virgin, c.1501
Tempera on wood

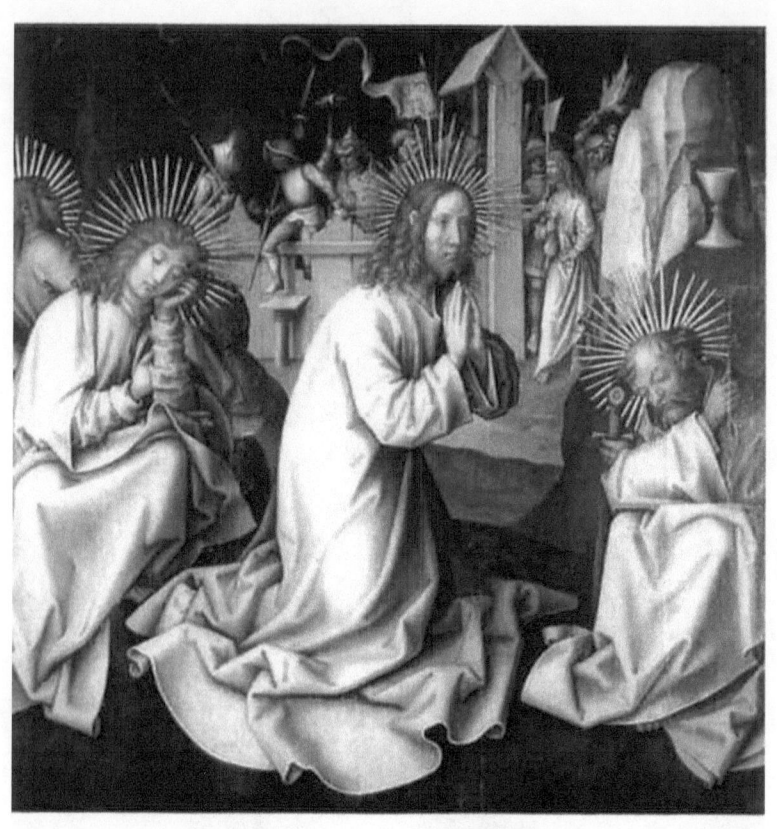

The Agony in the Garden, c.1505
Tempera on wood

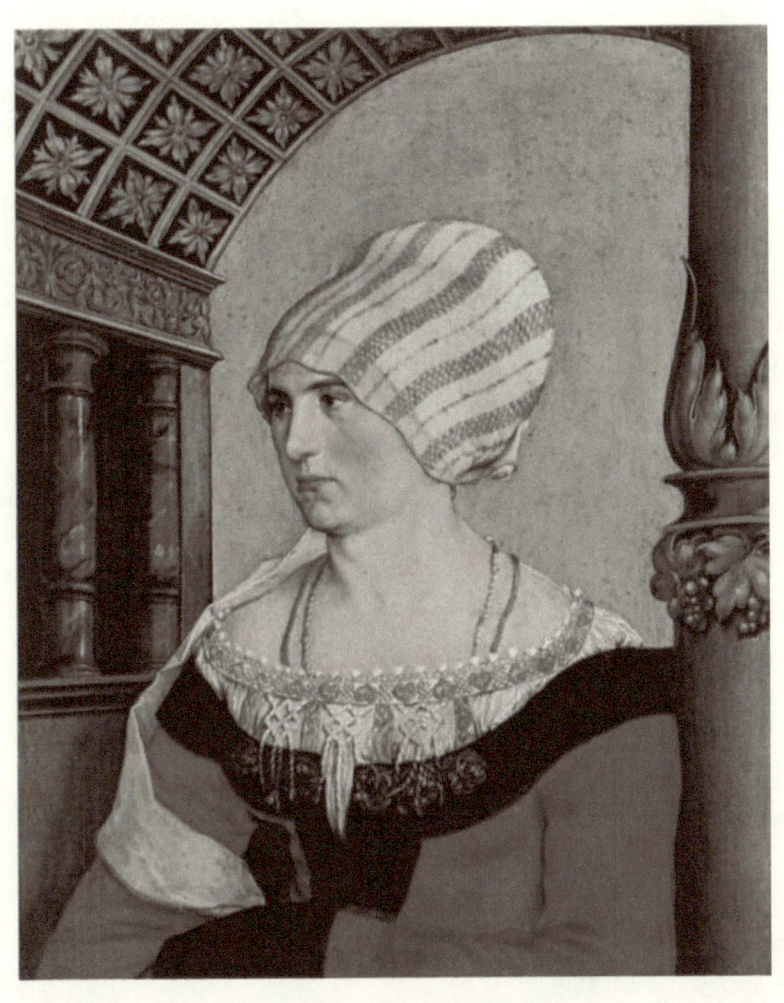

Dorothea Kannengiesser, 1516
Oil on panel

There is a companion-piece of this painting, the portrait of the sitter's husband, Jakob Meyer zum Hasen. The architecture provides a link between the two portraits and creates a shared space for the figures; prior to Holbein, such a pictorial concept was unknown in Basel panel painting. The same applies to the decorative elements on the architecture, derived from the Italian Renaissance, such as the coffered vault and the acanthus leaf frieze, which incorporates two putti.

The gilded coffering and pillar enhance the appearance of sober opulence in this striking and forthright depiction of Dorothea Kannengiesser, the second wife of Jakob Meyer. Their double-portrait, signed and dated 1516, was probably commissioned to celebrate Meyer's election as burgomaster. This had crucial repercussions for Holbein's career; evidently pleased with such an impressive diptych from so young an artist, Meyer gained Holbein numerous commissions in the following few years. Meyer was a member of the increasingly important mercantile class in Basel and the first of its members to achieve significant administrative power. (The coin he holds signifies his money-dealing role and also perhaps Basel's new-found permission to mint coins.) His friends and colleagues were therefore in the financial position to aid Holbein through their patronage. Meyer's tenure was brief, however - in 1521 he was impeached for accepting a larger bribe than was permitted from the French, imprisoned when he protested at his treatment and barred from office thereafter. He remained a Catholic after the city's secession to the reformed religion and led the Catholic party in the city: Holbein would perceive such strength of character again, in the analogous determination of Sir Thomas More to remain true to his faith.

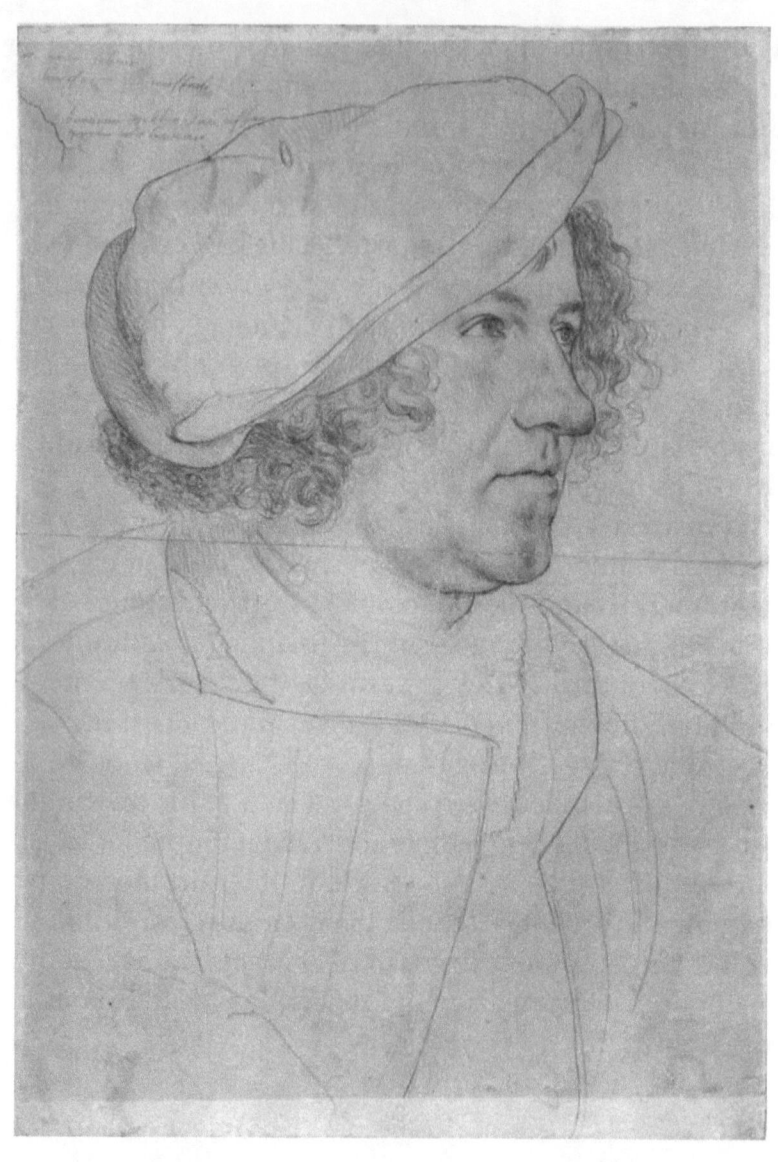

Portrait of Jakob Meyer zum Hasen, 1516
Silverpoint, red chalk, and traces of black pencil on
white coated pape

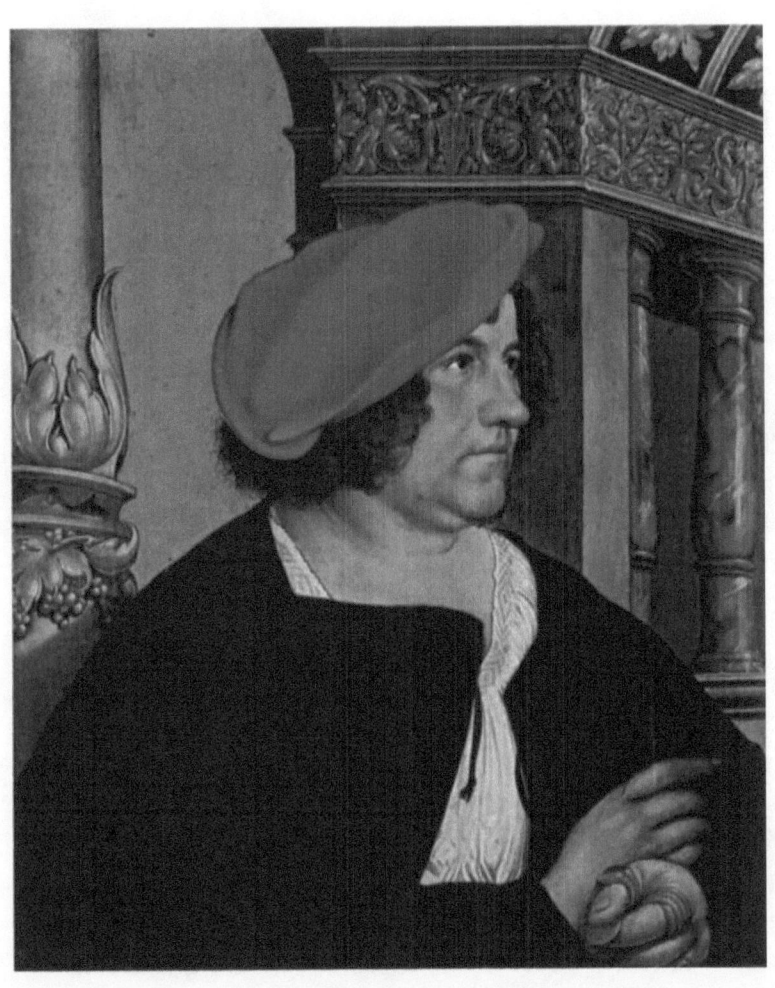

Mayor Jakob Meyer zum Hasen, 1516
Oil on wood

The transference of artistic knowledge and material from Italy northwards through the Alpine passes during the late fifteenth and early sixteenth century led to the emergence of Italianate portrait-construction in Germany. This was being practiced with increasing confidence by the time Holbein received his first commissions. Dьrer was crucial here, primarily through his Venetian visits in 1496-7 and 1506. Holbein eschewed most of the emotionalism intricately bound up in Dьrer's view of the world and once having developed his ability to make a calm appraisal of the sitter's condition, as demonstrated here, maintained it throughout his career. This has led to the mistaken belief that little or nothing changed in his technique over thirty-five years.

As a result of the power and poise of Holbein's preliminary silverpoint portrait, line dominates over colour and texture throughout the painting, except, ironically, in the face. The lines of the bunched fingers compel attention more against the undifferentiated dark jacket, and the illustrative rigour of the architectural background belies the subtlety of light and shadow in the face, perhaps revealing an overly self conscious borrowing of Italianate design at this early stage in the artist's career.

The portrait seems to have had a personal function, as the mayor and his wife are informally, if splendidly, dressed. Meyer's main concern would have been the proud display of his wealth, which had enabled this merchant's son to become the first mayor of Basel who was not from the city's upper class but a representative of the guilds. The coin that Meyer holds out prominently towards the viewer presumably refers first and foremost to his occupation as a moneychanger, and only secondarily to the right of the city of Basel, confirmed in 1516 by the Emperor Maximilian (emperor 1486-1519), to mint gold coins. The numerous gold rings on Mayer's left hand vividly demonstrate his prosperity. With his right index finger he points discreetly at his wife, who is likewise richly arrayed, in her case in pearls and gold chains, and clothes and bonnet that are expensively embroidered and laced with gold thread. Even the architecture - with its glossy columns of red veined marble, richly decorated frieze with classical acanthus leaves, and expensively coffered barrel vaulting borrowed from Italian Renaissance architecture - creates a splendid frame for the figures. Holbein places the self assured man in front of the solid pier, thus underlining his physical dominance vis-à-vis the petite woman, who is seated against a monochrome blue background.

In a small cartouche in the frieze above the head of Jakob Meyer, Hans Holbein has signed the double portrait with his initials and dated it 1516. This is the first time Holbein, still an apprentice painter, emerges from anonymity. The architecture provides a link between the two portraits and creates a shared space for the figures; prior to Holbein, such a pictorial concept was unknown in Basel panel painting. The same applies to the decorative elements on the architecture, derived from the Italian Renaissance, such as the coffered vault and the acanthus leaf frieze, which incorporates two putti.

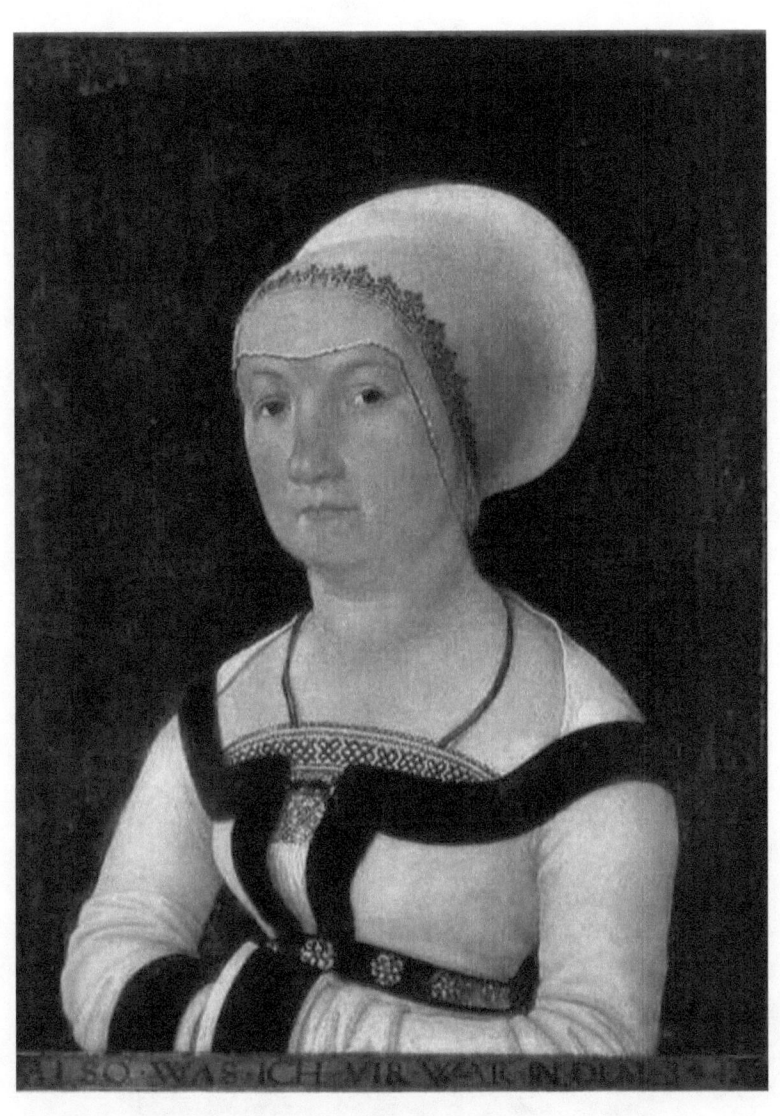

Portrait of 34 year old Woman, 1516
Tempera on wood

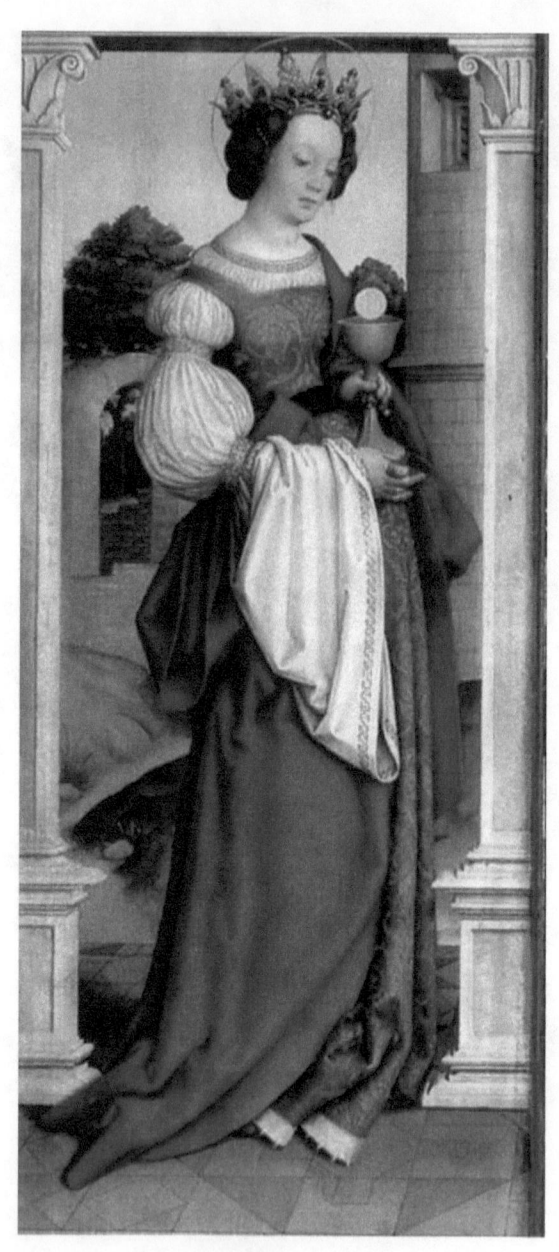

St Barbara, 1516
Tempera on wood

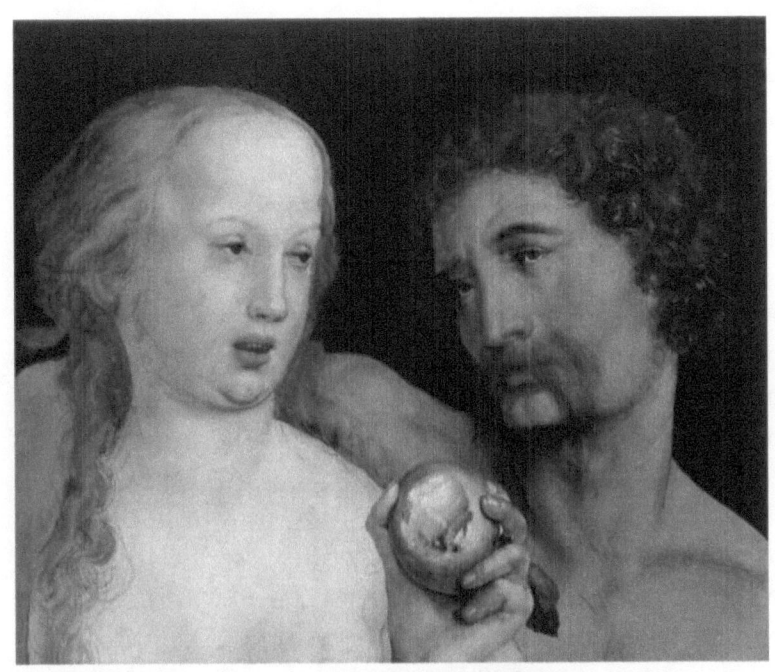

Adam and Eve, 1517
Tempera on wood

By 1515 Hans Holbein and his elder brother Ambrosius
had left Augsburg to establish them in Basel and were
travelling to nearby towns like Lucerne to carry out
commissions, often in journeymen teams. Their father,
Hans the Elder, was also involved in such projects.

Though no prodigy (he was nearly twenty when this work was done) Hans shows how he has already assimilated the contemporary `Swiss' style in the unidealised, thinly-painted figures, whose faces abound with pentimenti - such corrections can be seen around Adam's eyes. The strongly linear nature of his art is already evident in the fluid, abstracted line of Adam's shoulder. This is memorably combined with the telling realism of the worm-eaten apple Eve holds up to view. Such attention to transitory and corrupt nature (exemplified by Adam and Eve) was a frequent concern of artists in the German schools - Dьrer, Hans Baldung Grien and Grьnewald. The emotional tone, of regret and world-weariness, is established with considerable subtlety in the faces of the transgressing couple, without the melodrama of much contemporary work, and presages the mature Holbein's psychological insight.

Adam and Eve are painted as busts and are set against a flat black background. This choice of representation is reminiscent of half length portraits, especially as the features of the first human couple are scarcely idealized and therefore seem more portrait-like. This is Holbein's way of individualizing the subject of the Fall of Man. The painting cannot have served as a devotional picture, since Adam and Eve were not saints and could not be invoked as intercessors. The picture must therefore have been intended for private religious meditation.

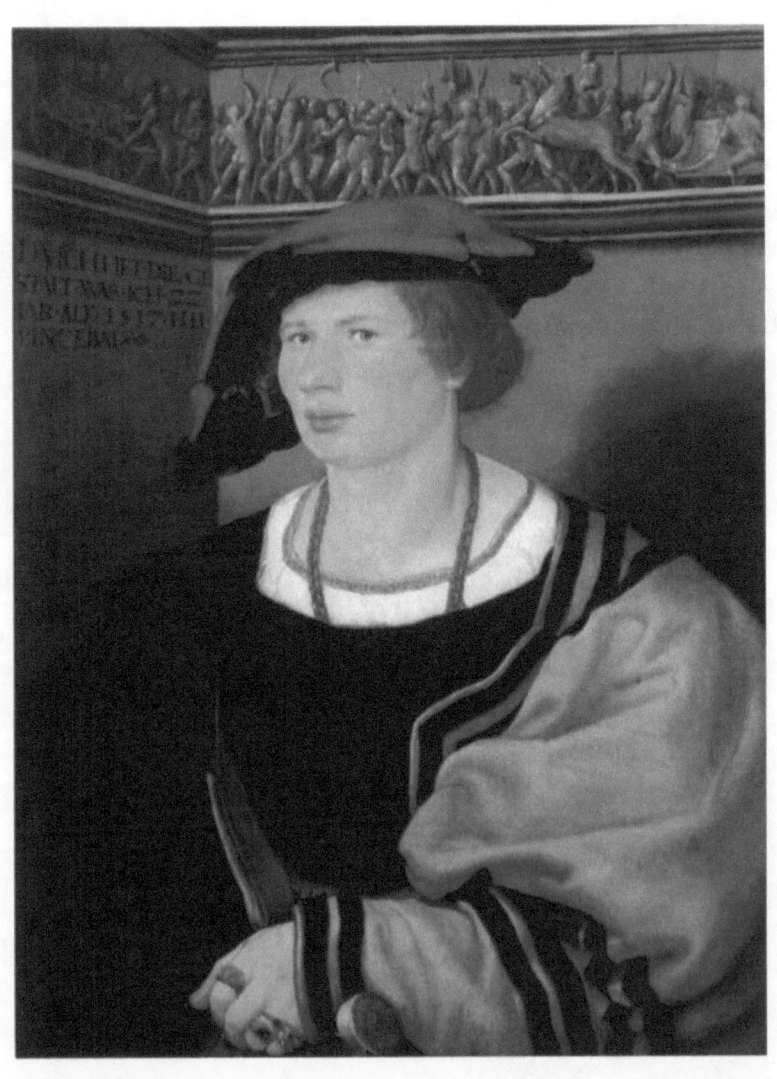

Portrait of Benedikt von Hertenstein, 1517
Oil on wood

The German inscription on the wall proclaims that the sitter is 22 and looks exactly like his portrait. This is said in direct speech, as if Benedikt von Hertenstein, who turns and looks directly at the viewer, were himself speaking. The reference is to the astounding verisimilitude of the portrait, a theme that can be traced back to antiquity. Holbein also adds succinctly, in Latin, that he painted the portrait in 1517.

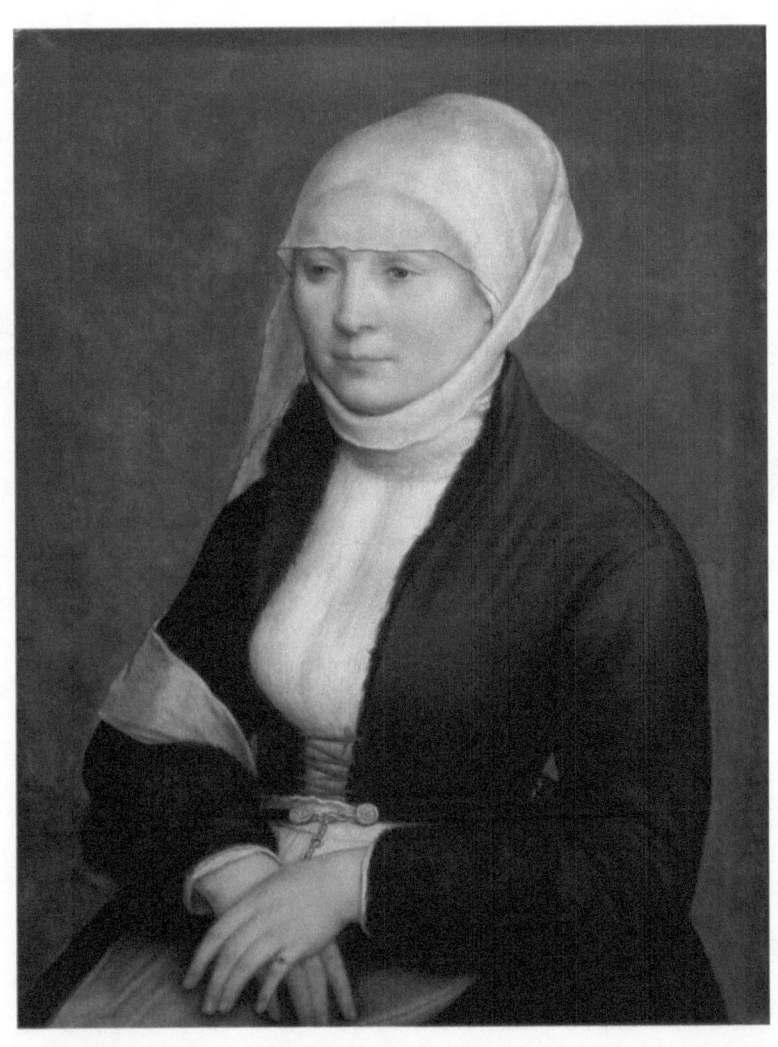

Presumed Portrait of the Artist's Wife, c.1517
Tempera on wood

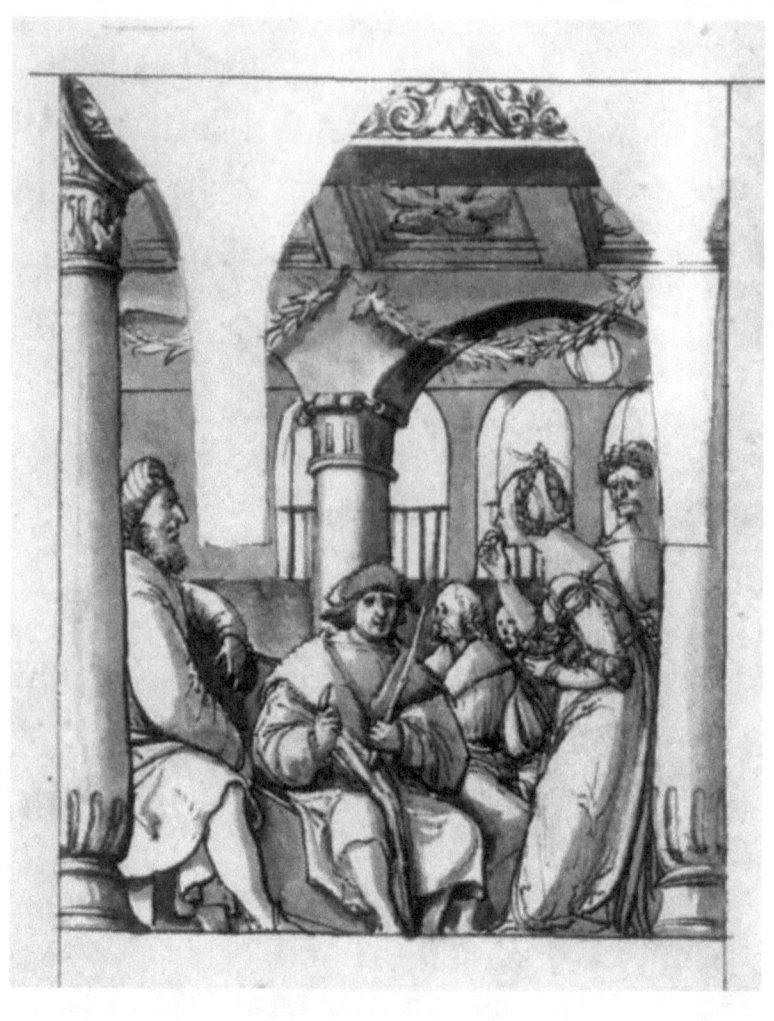

Leaina before the Judges
1517-18, Pen and brush in black and gray, with gray
wash

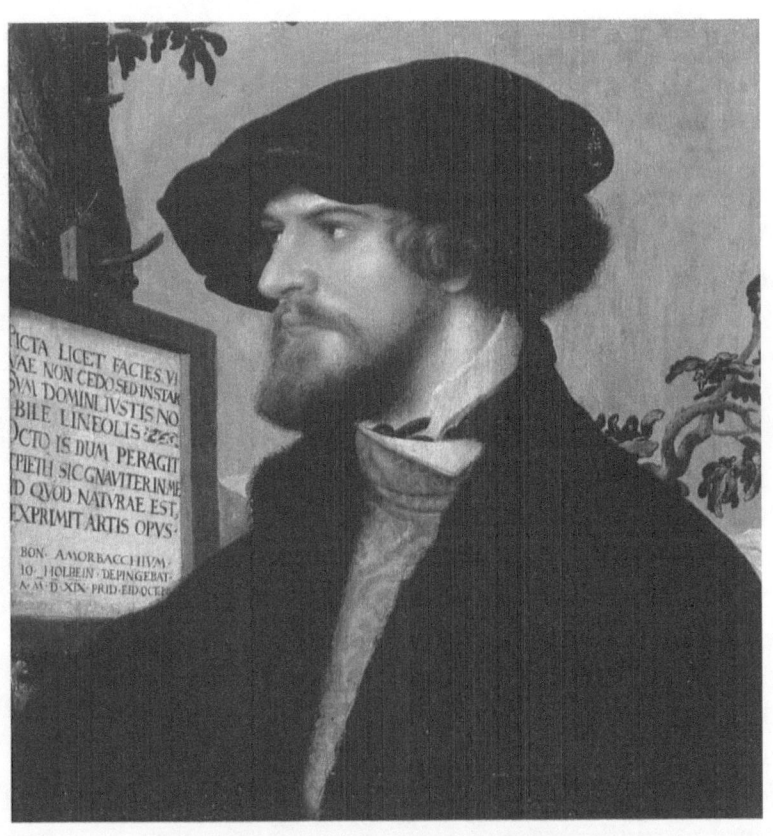

Portrait of Bonifacius Amerbach, 1519
Oil on wood

Bonifacius Amerbach (1495-1562) studied both law and classical antiquity in Basel and then Freiburg. In 1520 he went to Avignon to continue his studies under the writer, lawyer, and music theoretician Andreas Alciatus (1492-1550), known as Alciat. In 1525, Amerbach finally gained a chair in Roman law at the important university of Basel. His distinctive position as a scholar is revealed by his friendship with Erasmus, who named him as his sole heir. Like Bonifacius Amerbach, his son Basilius also became a passionate collector of Holbein's works, collecting them in the "Amerbach Cabinet," which later formed the core of Basel's art museum.

The year 1519 was marked by civic success for Holbein; he was made a Master in the painters' guild `zum Himmel', took up Basel citizenship and married. Until this date much of his daily work had been for the decorative arts, particularly glass-painting and book-illustration, but a new emphasis on portraiture, fomented by the success of the Meyer commission, first emerges with this piece.

Holbein was lucky to have Amerbach as a friend and patron; the dogged and determined gaze of the withal kindly scholar, eventually Professor of Law at the university, was to be borne out in his assiduous collecting of Holbein's Basel oeuvre.

The work is more painterly than the Meyer double-portrait and uses classical references with more confidence, as is appropriate in a portrayal of Amerbach in academic black. The panel bears Amerbach's own words of praise for the artist's truthfulness to nature and it also serves, pictorially, to emphasize the depth of illusory picture-space. As a result sitter and background are well-integrated, and real poetic feeling is glimpsed in the distant snow-covered mountains and chill blue sky.

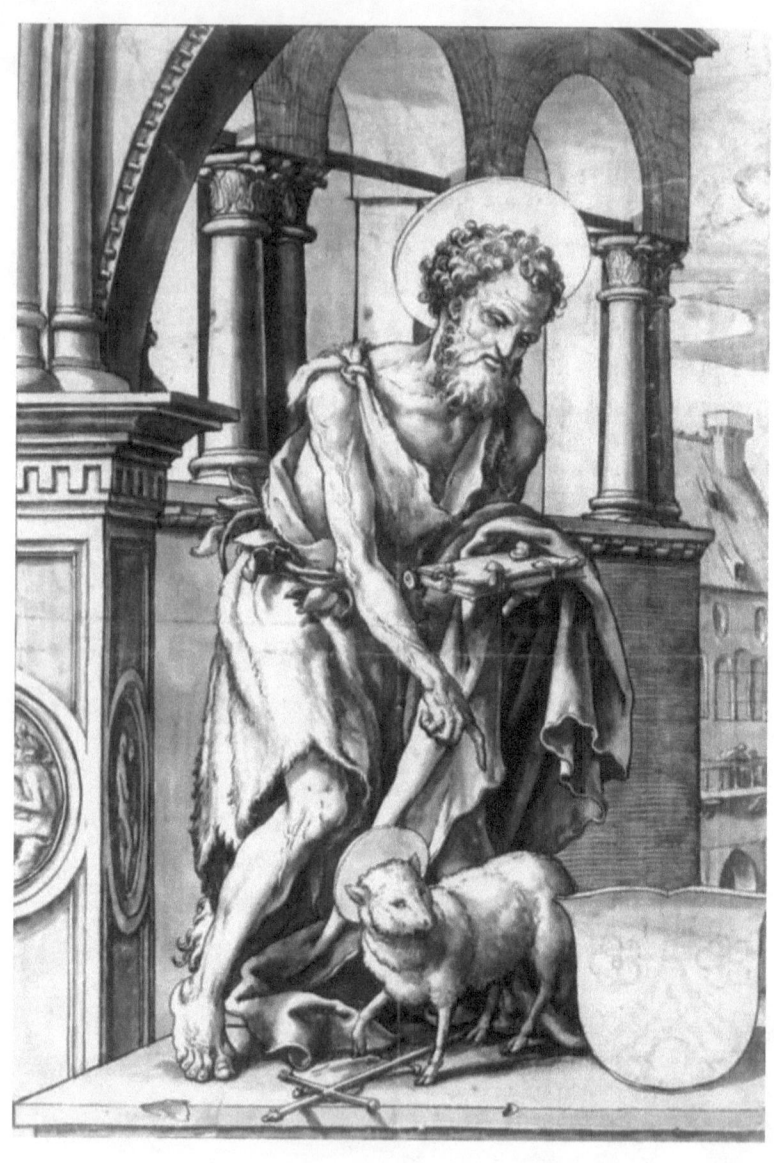

St John the Baptist, 1519-20
Pen and black ink on a chalk sketch, with a gray wash

This drawing comes from a series of eight in the Basel Kupferstichkabinett (engravings collection). Holbein probably drew them as cartoons for four pairs of windows in a church in Basel, and they clearly illustrate his close involvement in the manufacture of stained glass. That this drawing was a study for stained glass is clearly shown by the drawing technique - dark strokes of the pen emphasize the contours, there is an absence of hatching, and the forms are modeled by washes. The lively play of the hems of the garments, and powerful, expressive wash are typical of the young Holbein.

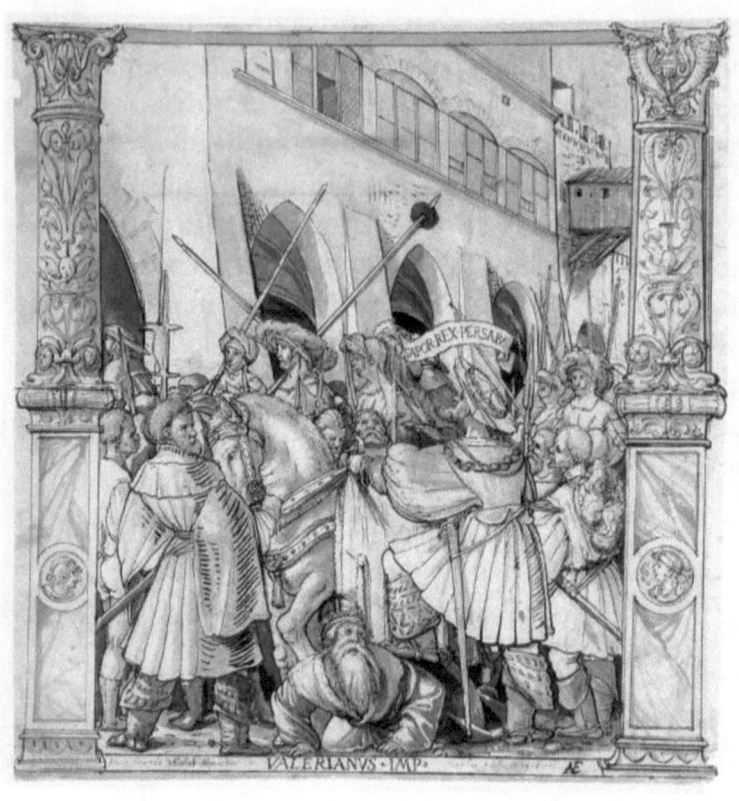

The Humiliation of the Emperor Valerian by the
Persian King Sapor, c. 1521
Pen and black ink on chalk sketch, gray wash and
watercolour,

Finalized in 1521, the program of murals for the Great Council Chamber of Basel Town Hall consisted of the Virtues and scenes from antiquity. A scene intended to remind councilors not to misuse their power shows the humiliation of Valerian. This Roman emperor was shamefully treated by the victorious king of the Persians, Sapor, who, after his victory at Edessa, used the emperor as a stool to mount his horse. As it was a scene rarely illustrated, Holbein provided the names of the main characters as inscriptions.

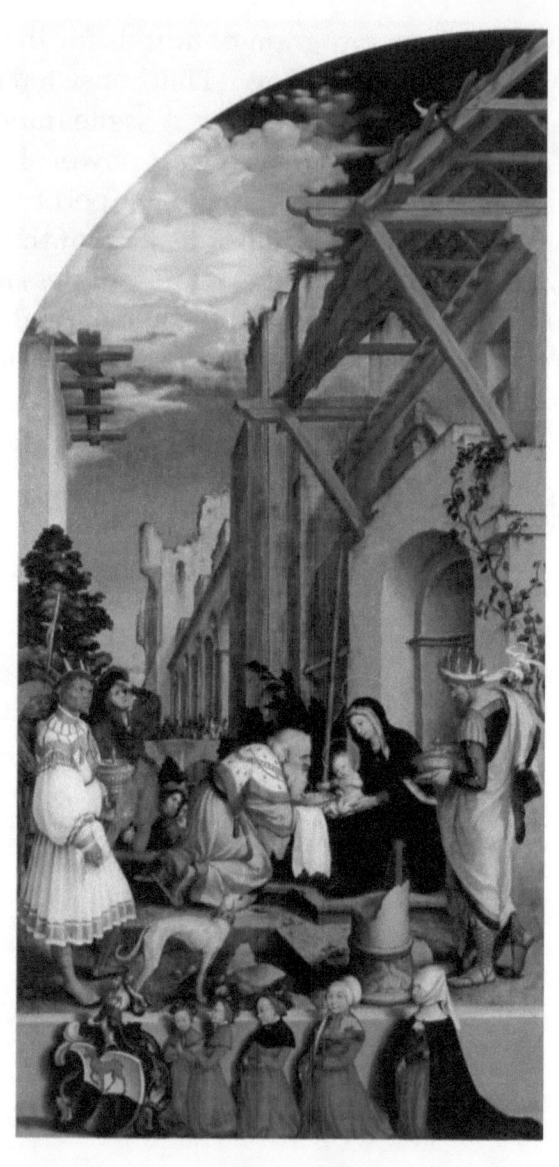

Oberried Altarpiece, left interior wing - The Adoration
of the Magi, 1522
Tempera on wood

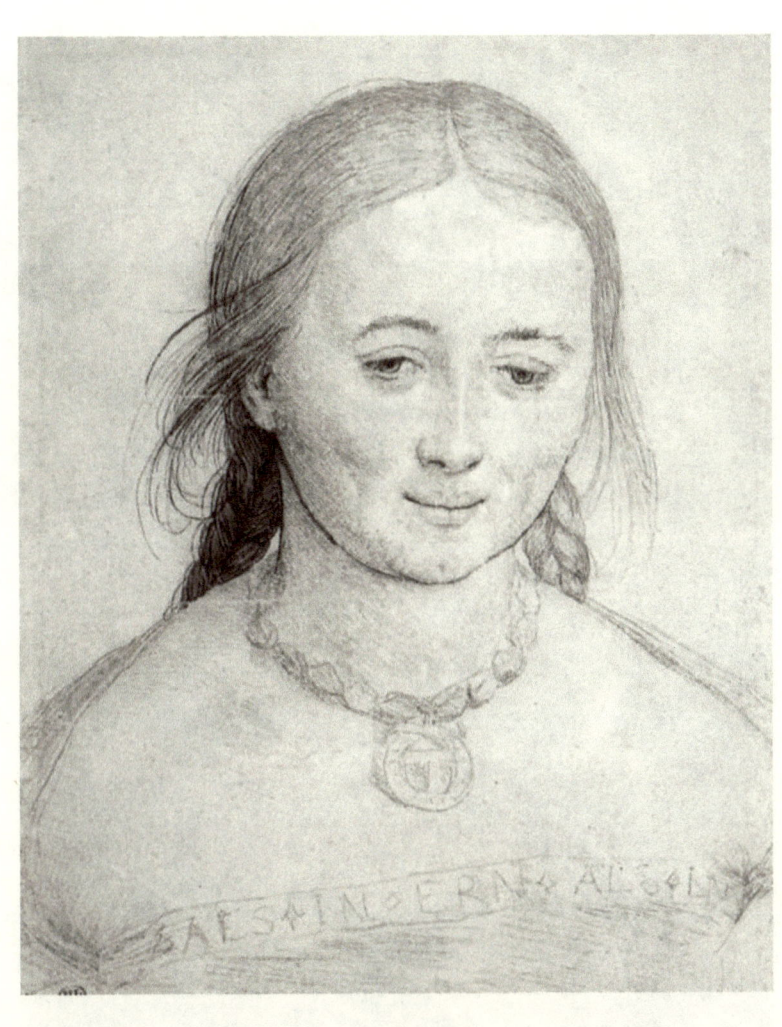

Head of a Woman, 1522
Drawing

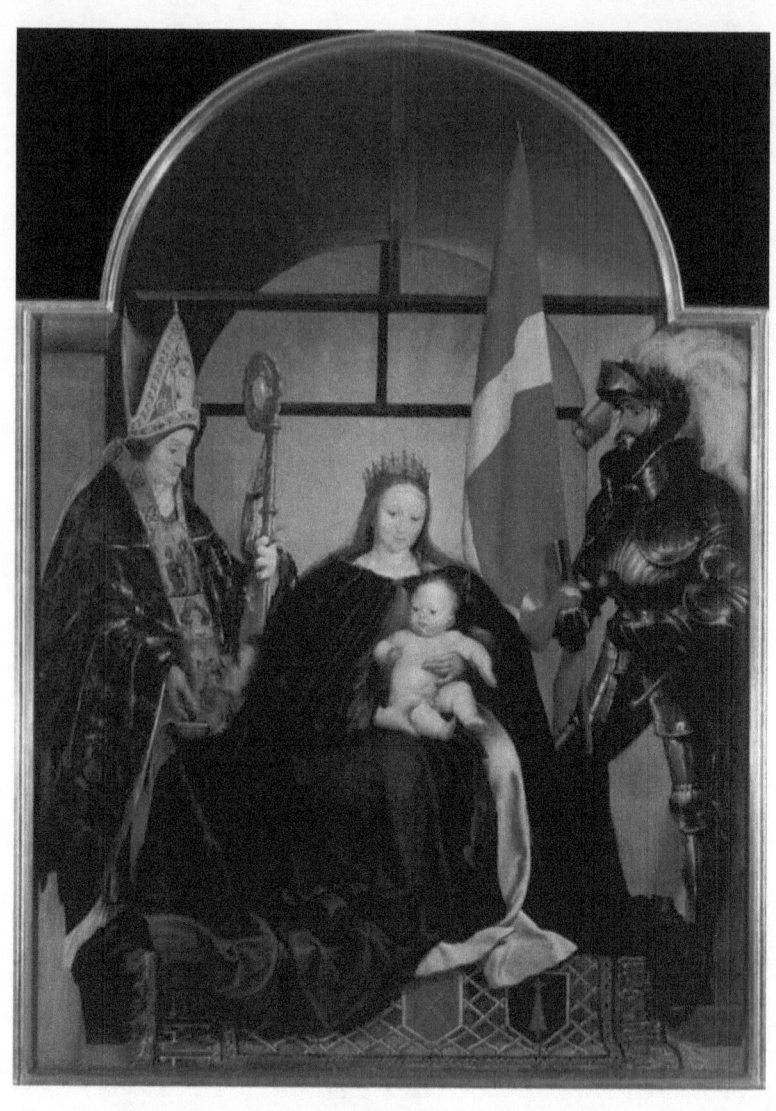

The Solothurn Madonna, 1522
Limewood

The commission came from the city clerk of Basel, Johannes Gerster, and his wife Barbara Guildinknopf. The couple's coats of arms are woven into the cloth that covers the steps of the throne, which is also where Holbein signed and dated his work. The work is a sacra conversazione, a popular form of Madonna favoured in Upper Italy, especially by Bellini and Giorgione and their circles, where the Virgin is depicted almost always sitting or standing centrally and is flanked by saints. Holbein's composition enables praying believers to address the Virgin and Saints Martin and Ursus with the confidence that their intercession with God will grant the faithful the certainty of salvation. The Virgin looks at the viewers with a kindly gaze and gently inclined head, presenting to them the Christ Child, who raises His hand in a childlike blessing.

The Madonna sits beneath a bare tunnel vault, flanked by two saints. The figure on the left, the bishop giving alms to a beggar, is St Martin. The knight in armor, whose only attribute is a red flag with a white cross held in his right hand, must be St Ursus. The minster in Solothurn is dedicated to him, and he is also venerated in St Martin's in Basel. The picture must have been intended for this church, where the man who commissioned the picture, Johannes Gerster, was provisor.

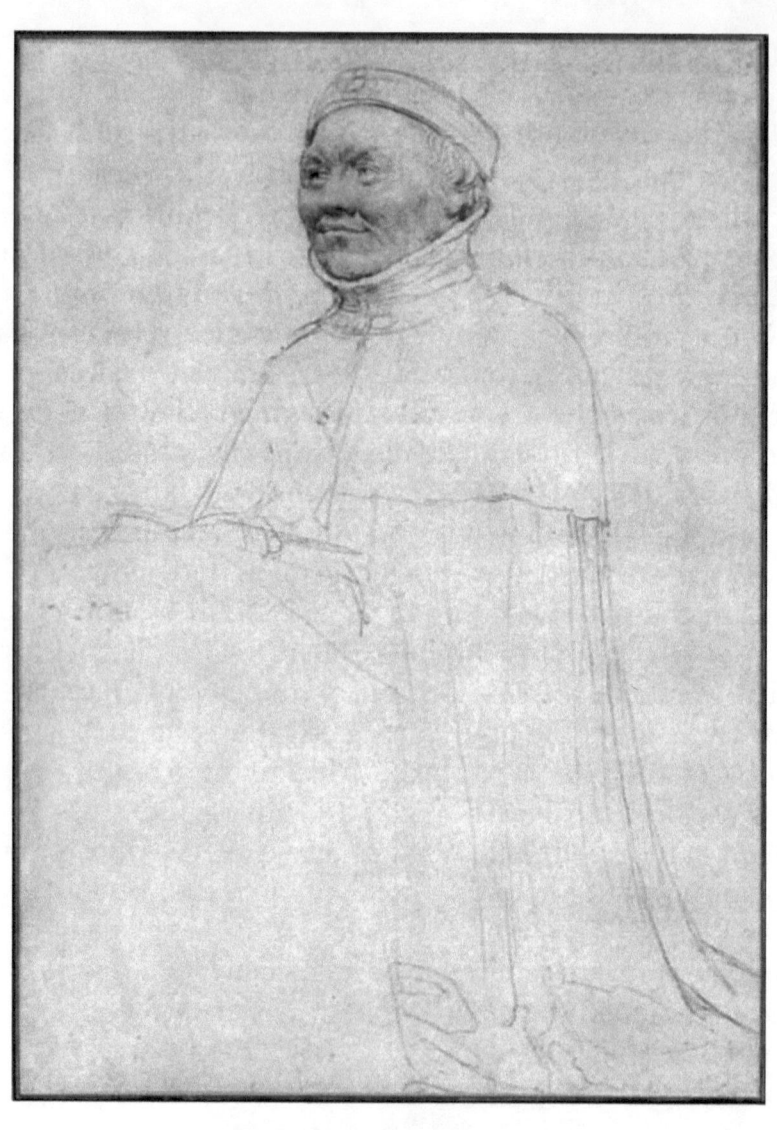

Duc Jean de Berry, 1522
Chalk drawing

Duc Jean de Berry (1340-1416) was the most famous art patron of the Gothic age and commissioner of several important manuscripts including the Trϻs Belles Heures de Notre-Dame du Duc de Berry.

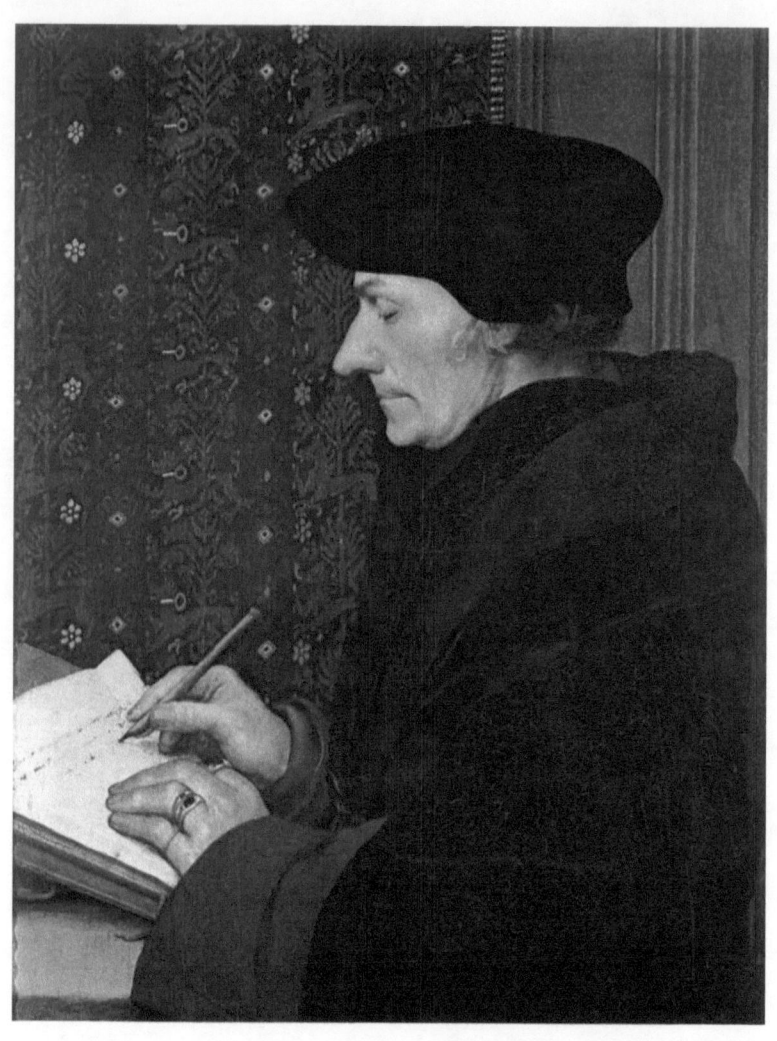

Portrait of Desiderius Erasmus, 1523
Oil on panel

The painting shows Erasmus writing the first lines of
his "Comments on the Gospel of St Luke" dated 1523.
The lines are not legible on this painting but it is legible
on another smaller version of the portrait in the
museum of Basel.

As in the Basel portrait, Holbein here depicts Erasmus as the learned author actively pursuing his vocation as a writer - his gaze is lowered and he focuses entirely on the text he is writing. Even though the scholar's study chambers is not shown, the tapestry with its pattern of plants and fabulous beasts and the wooden paneling explicitly indicate, unlike the background of the Basel version, that this is an interior.

Holbein's greatness is demonstrated in this fine portrait not only in its technical mastery but also in its comprehension and presentation of the salient features of the subject's personality and activity. The scale of Erasmus' bulk within the picture space is prodigious; previously, scholars had been portrayed in book-lined studies, surrounded by the tools of their trade, musing as does Saint Jerome in Dьrer's woodcut of 1514, complete with shaggy lion. (Erasmus himself edited Saint Jerome's works, thus identifying with the patron saint of translators.) Saint Augustine was also popularly depicted in a monastic study, as in Carpaccio's appealing image of 1505.

Holbein's treatment is more intimate; to be able to look over the scholar's shoulder at the pen poised on the paper (engaged on the Paraphrase of Saint Mark) is an honour the nervous Erasmus would have granted only to intellectual equals. It has been concluded that Sir Thomas More was the intended recipient of this version: Erasmus was usually posed in a more formal three-quarter view. Such portraits were often exchanged by humanists as tokens of mutual esteem, which explains the considerable number of painted and engraved copies in existence; aspiring scholars would use these to adorn their studies as encouragement to their emulatory efforts.

Erasmus lived through writing and above all, by correspondence; ironically, in 1533 he was to censure Holbein for delaying in Antwerp which was preventing Erasmus' mail being delivered (Holbein being the bearer). Here, as in other portraits of him, we see the great master of North European humanism in his self appointed role as educational conscience of the age.

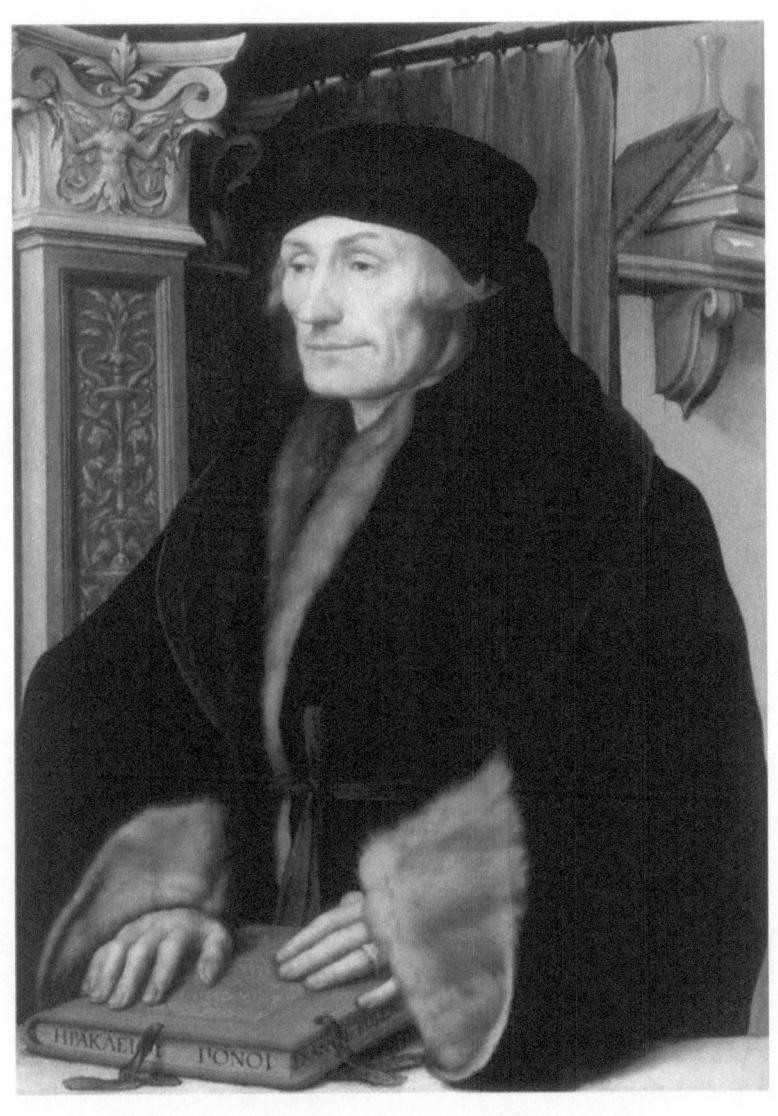

Portrait of Erasmus of Rotterdam, 1523
Oil on panel

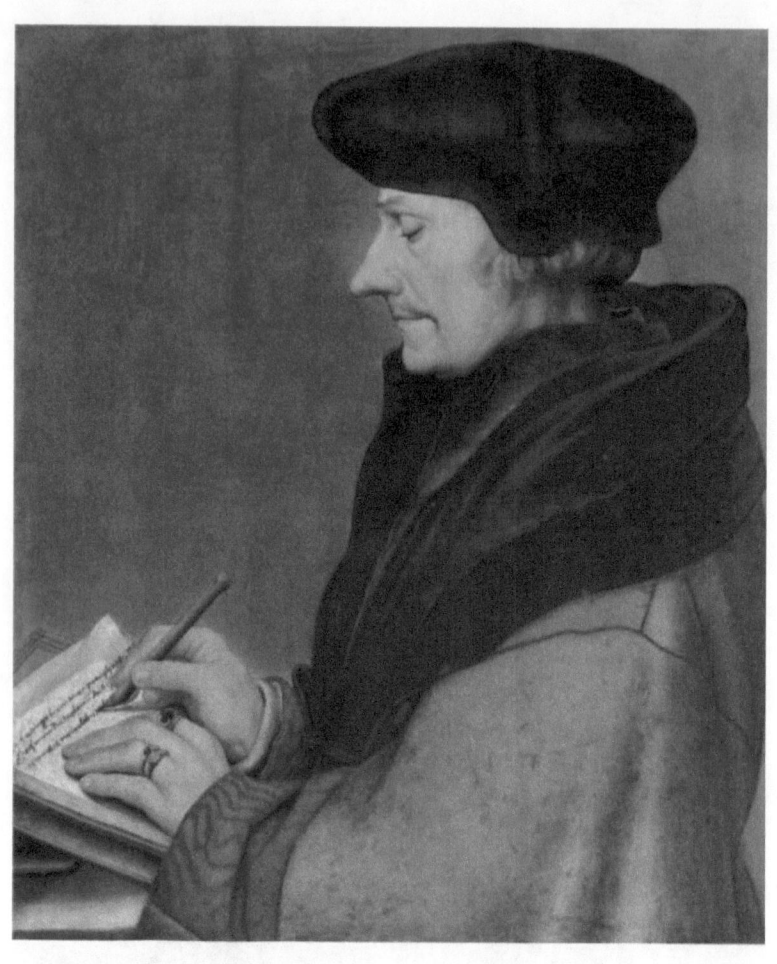

Portrait of Erasmus of Rotterdam Writing, 1523
Oil on panel

Born in Rotterdam in Holland in 1469, Erasmus entered the monastery of Steyn as an 18-year-old and was ordained in 1492. Following extensive studies in Paris, he became a Doctor of Theology in 1506. In Holbein's portrait, the 54-year-old Erasmus is shown wearing not a monk's cowl but the black robes of a scholar: in 1517 Pope Leo X had granted him the special privilege of not wearing monastic garments.

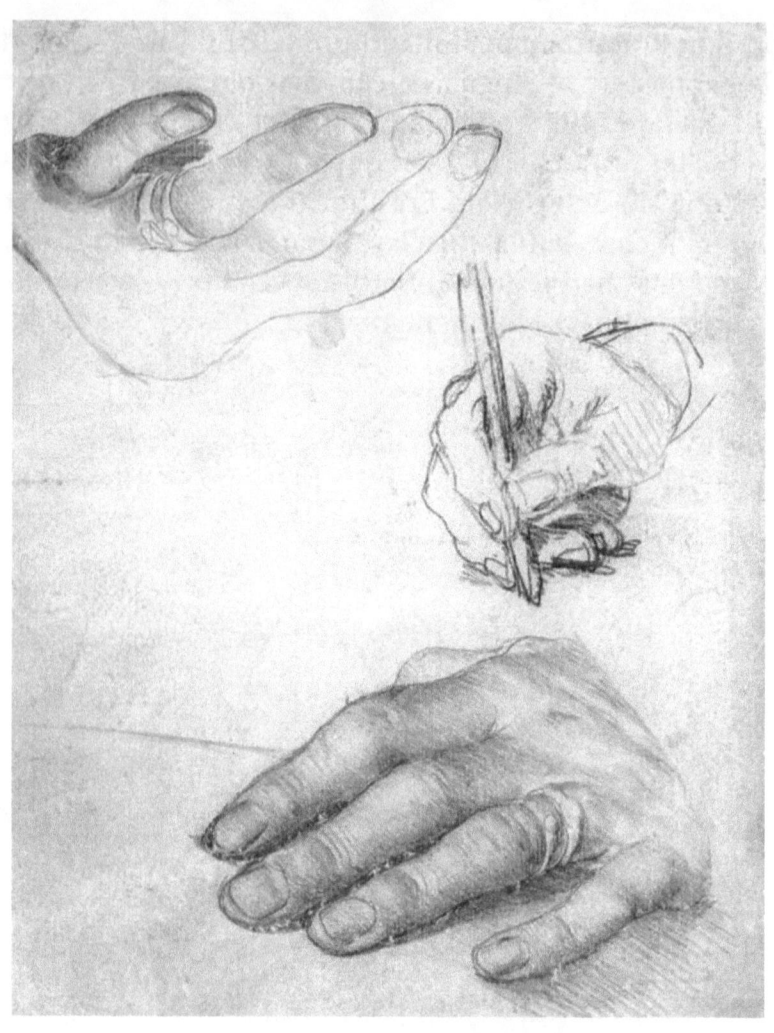

Studies of the Hands of Erasmus of Rotterdam, c. 1523
Silverpoint, ruddle, and black chalks on white coated
paper

Holbein's only known drawing of hand studies was executed as preparation for the Erasmus portraits. The artist shows the left hand in two slightly differing views, though the one at the top of the sheet was not completed, possibly because it was rejected. The lower one, worked out in great detail in silverpoint, supplied the model for corresponding hand of the Erasmus portrait in the Radnor Collectio. The right hand, which is shown, holding a pen, is only quickly sketched in black chalk. It is clearly the writing hand of the Paris and Basel versions, though the viewpoint was changed in the paintings.

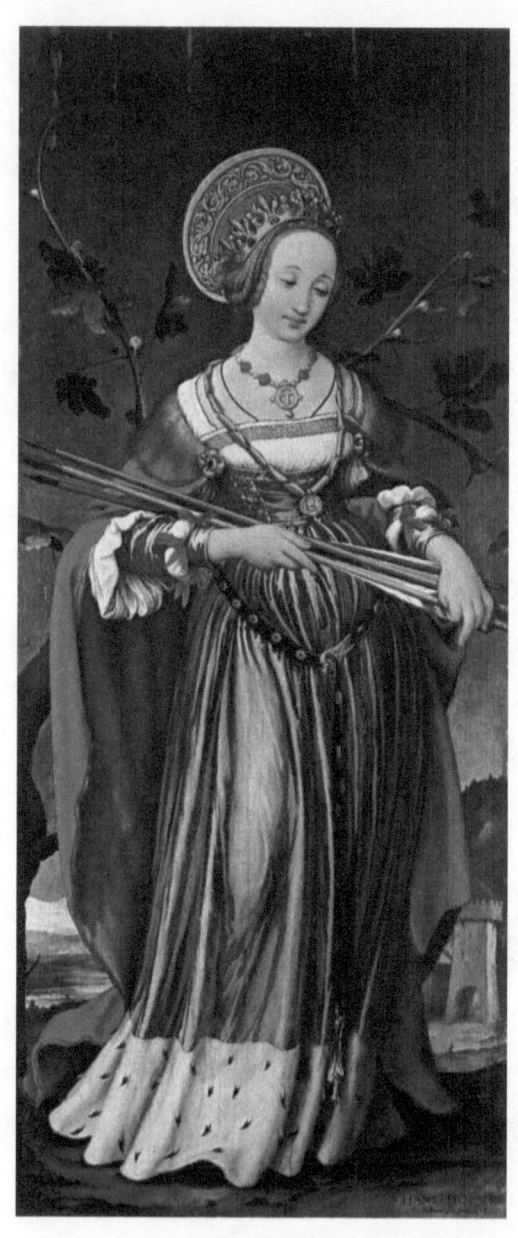

St. Ursula, c.1523
Tempera on panel

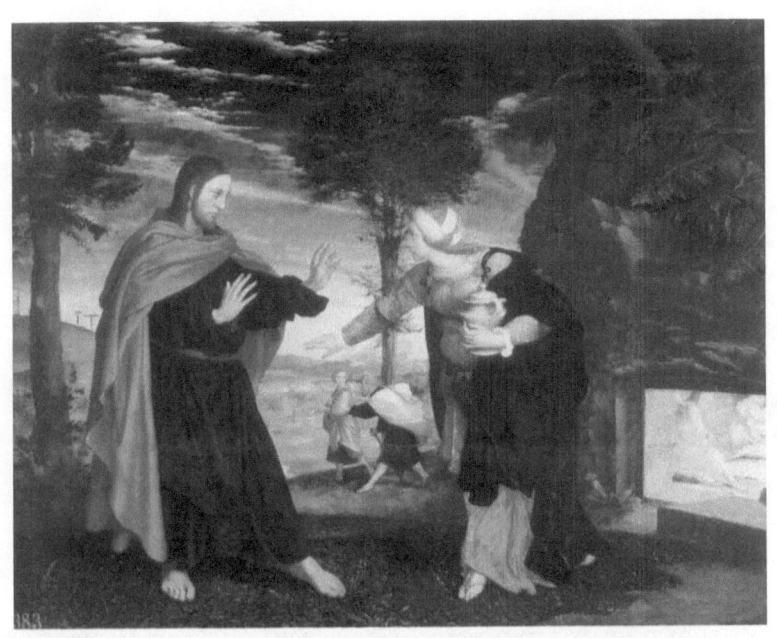

Noli me Tangere, 1524
Oil on wood

This Renaissance subject allowed the artists to explore
the theme of human emotion proffered and supra-
humanly rejected. Holbein's style is subtly different
here from his other religious work of the early 1520s. It
is more graceful, if somewhat awkwardly composed,
and has an air of mystery.

The Christ is akin to the melancholic long-faced figure in the Passion, but the chiaroscuro in the figures and their grace suggests some Leonardesque influence, if only second-hand. The profile of Mary Magdalene, the elegant phial she holds and her twisting pose are reminiscent of the figure style current in France, which Holbein visited at this time searching unsuccessfully for employment. It is probable that, adapt their conventions as he might, the robust, realist vein in Holbein seemed archaic to the sophisticates at King Francis I's court, who were to find the Italian Mannerism of Rosso Fiorentino much more to their taste in the following decade.

The emphatic drama of Holbein's account can be contrasted with the more elegiac quality of light, the landscape, more tempered poses and slighter figures in Titian's rendering.

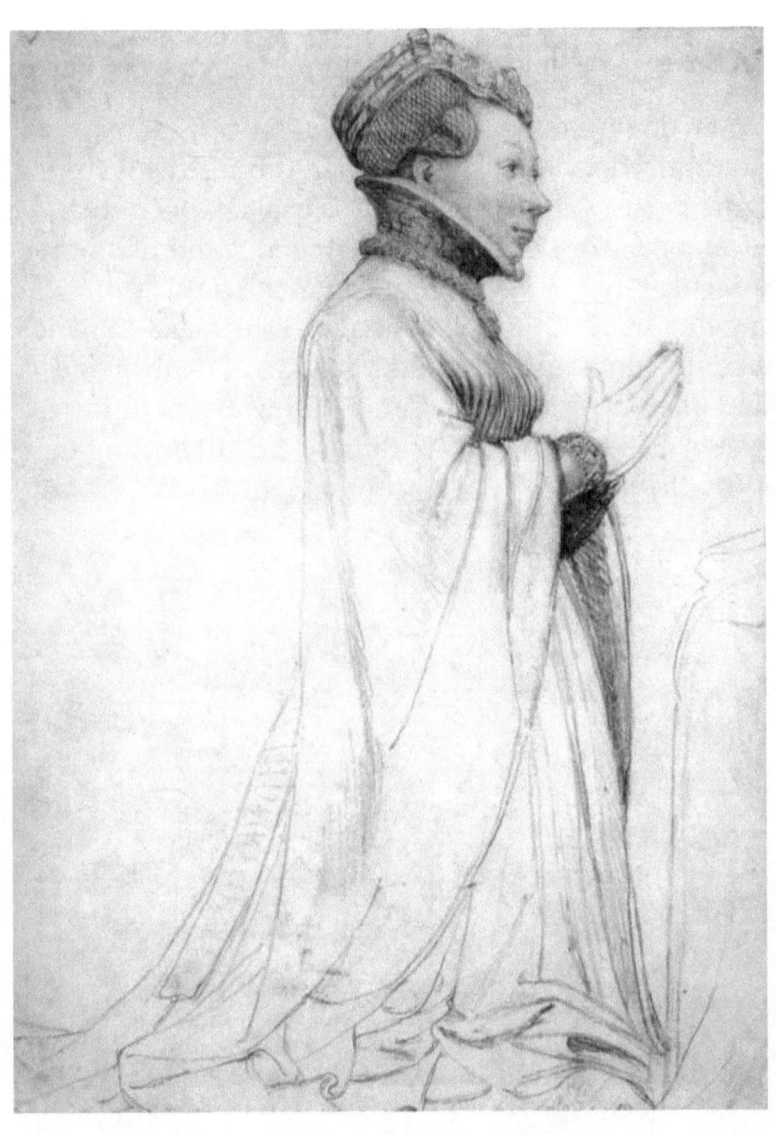

Jeanne de Boulogne, Duchess of Berry, 1524
Black and coloured chalks

During his visit to France, Holbein drew the sculpted figures of Duc Jean de Berry (1340-1416) and his wife Jeanne de Boulogne, probably sculpted by Jean de Cambrai (died 1438) after 1416. In the 16th century the figures were still in the private burial chapel of the ducal palace in Bourges. Holbein endeavours to bring the sculptures to life by colourings the flesh and drawing in additional details such as eyelashes, which of course the sculptor could not show. It was in effect a kind of competition between painting and sculpture, known as the paragone, with Holbein attempting to outdo the latter in verisimilitude.

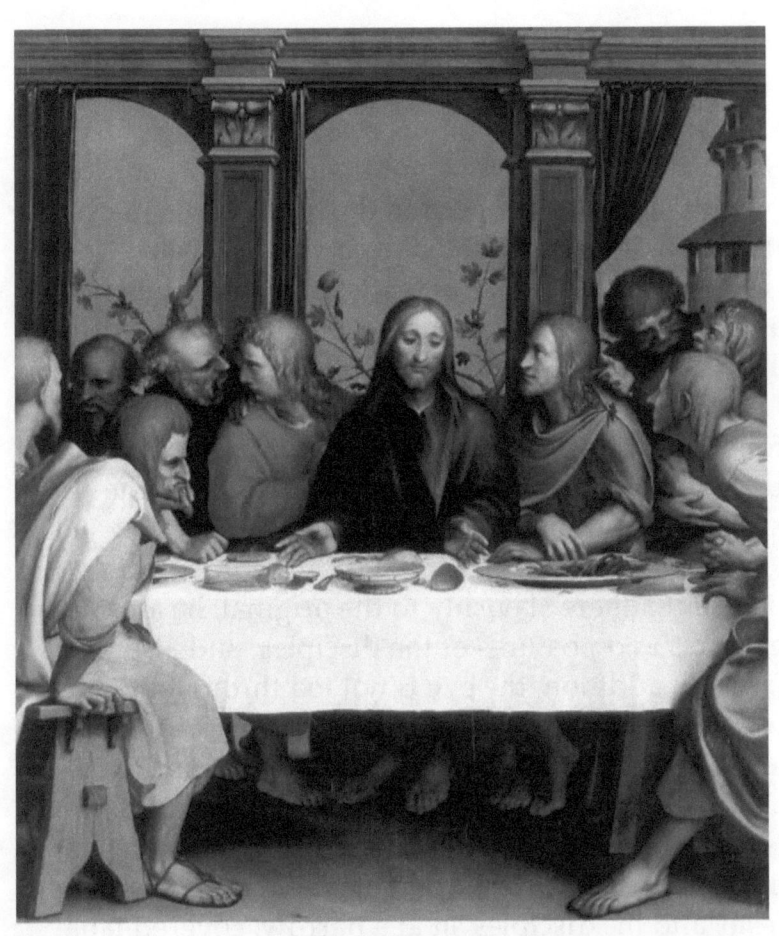

The Last Supper, 1524-25
Limewood

As was recognized very early by art historians, the composition of Holbein's Last Supper was based on Leonardo da Vinci's famous mural in the refectory of Santa Maria delle Grazie in Milan. As in Leonardo's picture, in Holbein's version the back wall is pierced by three windows, with the central window being reserved for the figure of Christ; the position of heads and arms also corresponds to Leonardo's composition. The dramatic interpretation likewise follows Leonardo's, the subject of the picture being the moment following Christ's announcement that He will soon be betrayed by one of them: as in the Leonardo, the apostles are animatedly discussing the shocking words Christ has just spoken. But, typically for Holbein, he does not adhere slavishly to the original; he alters the gestures and postures of the disciples, and also their faces. In addition, the eye is not led through the window openings to a distant landscape; Holbein encloses the shallow pictorial space by an intense blue sky that looks completely ethereal. The picture format is also more compact than Leonardo's, requiring a much more compressed arrangement of the figures. Jesus and his disciples sit at a narrow, covered table celebrating the Last Supper, but only nine of the twelve apostles are present. The three missing figures were possibly shown on the edges of the picture, which were lost when the panels were attacked in the iconoclastic riots of Reformation Basel, when the head of Christ was sawn out of the picture. The inventory of the Amerbach collection notes critically that the "supper on wood" was "coarsely" glued together.

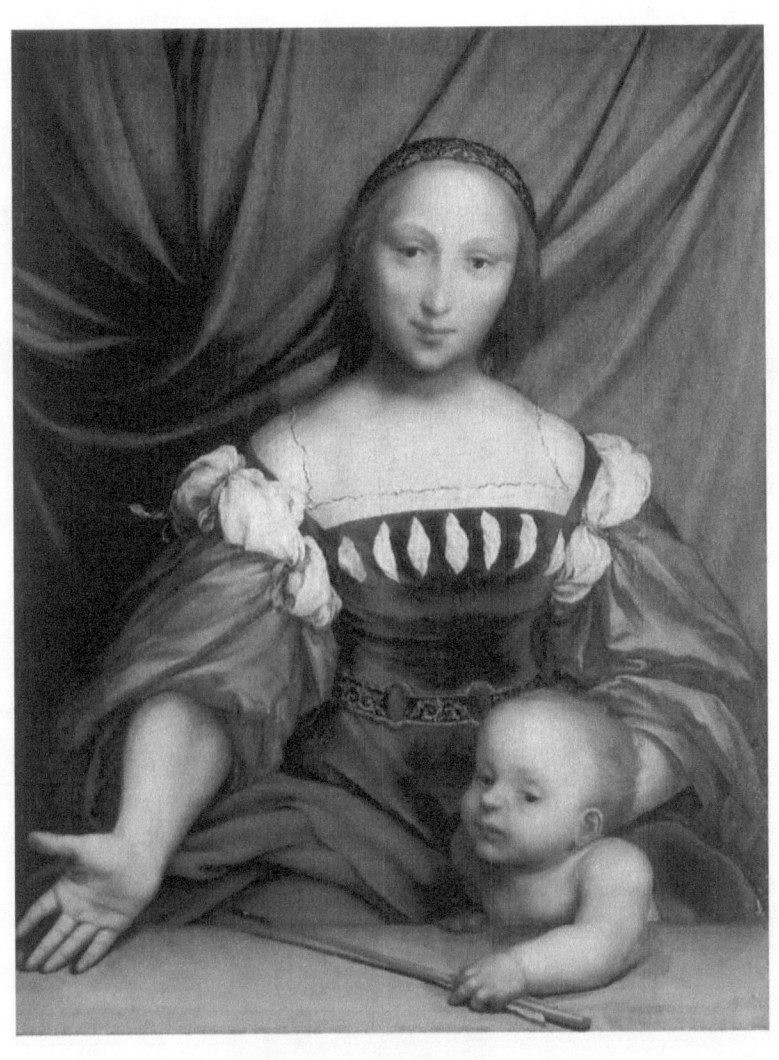

Venus and Amor, 1524-25
Limewood

Sitting in front of a green curtain and behind a low parapet, Venus, the Roman goddess of love, addresses the viewer with an open gesture and frank gaze. On her lap is the small, naked figure of Amor, who, holding love's arrow in his hand, is endeavouring to clamber on to the parapet.

It is not known who commissioned this picture, which is the earliest of Holbein's mythological paintings; it is first mentioned as being in the possession of Basilius Amerbach, who obtained it in 1578 as a present from his cousin, Franz Rechburger. In his inventory, Amerbach notes that the panels with Venus and Laïs are in fact portraits of a woman from the Offenburg family. However, even if Holbein did make use of a portrait study, he has idealized his model to the point where it can no longer be considered a true portrait.

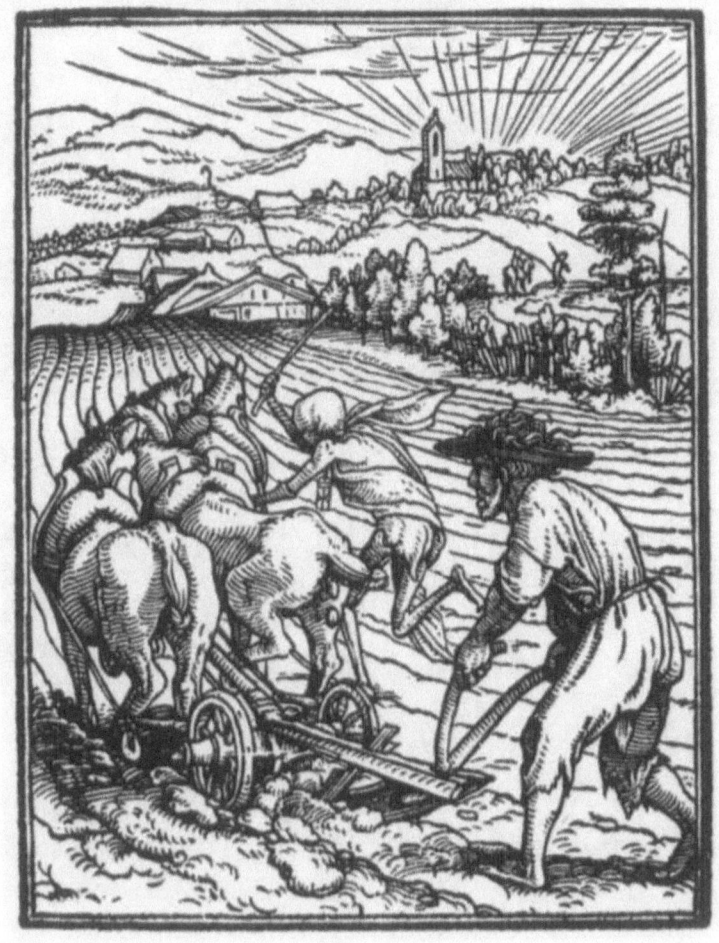

The Plowman from Dance of Death, 1524-26
Woodcut

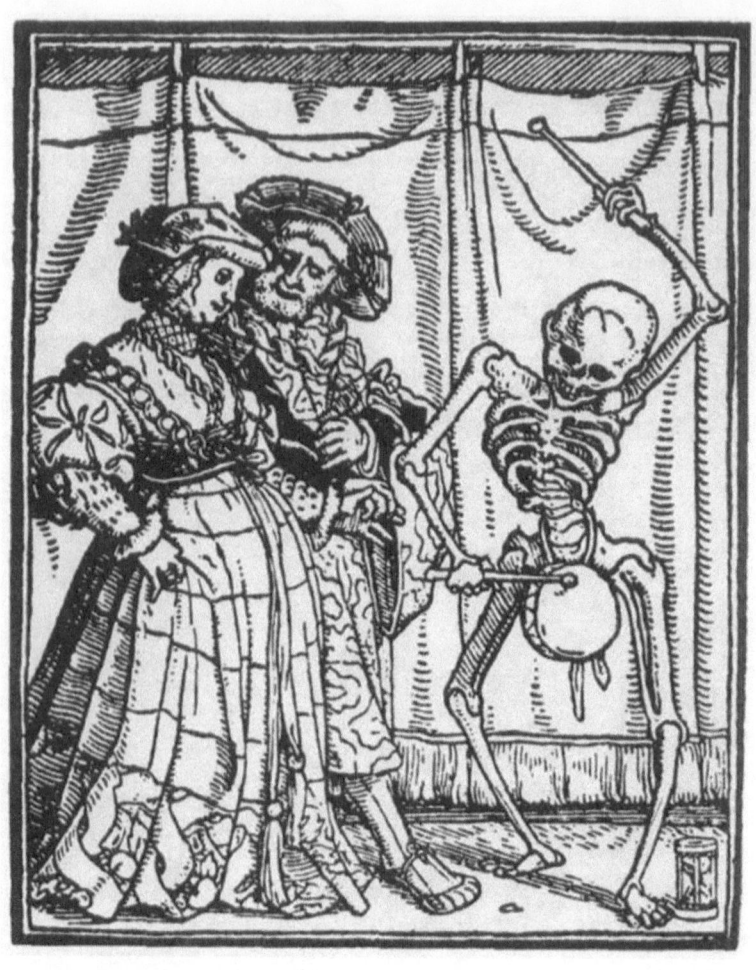

The Noble Lady from Dance of Death, 1524-26
Woodcut

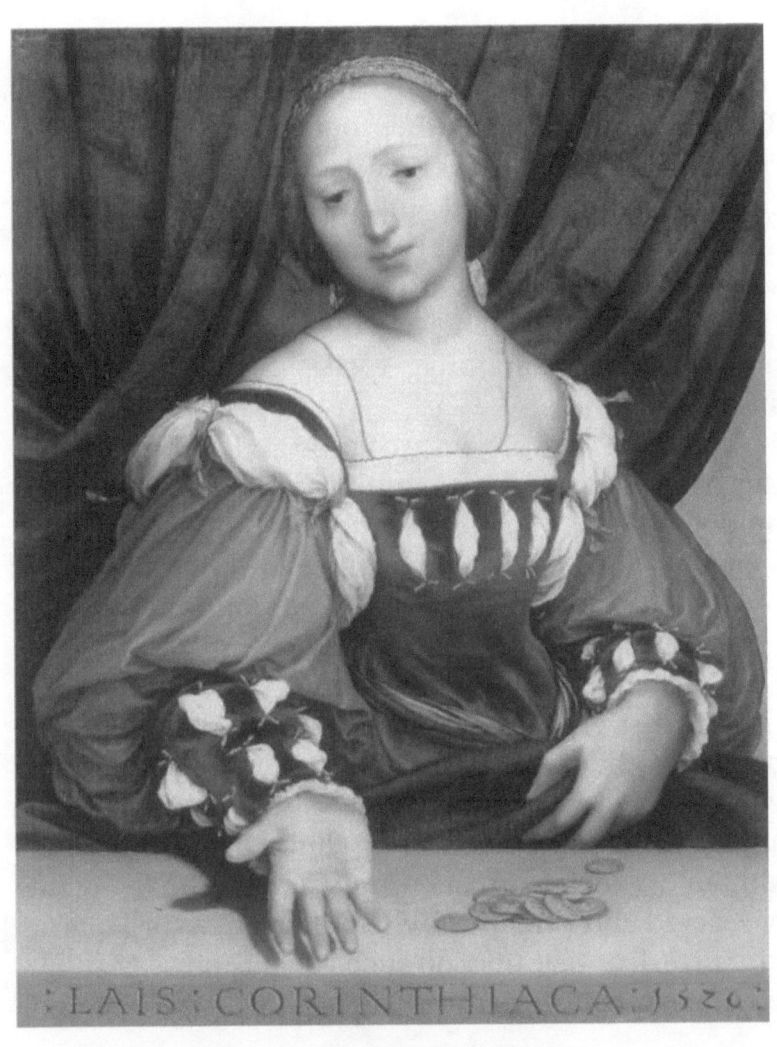

Lais Corinthiaca, 1526
Oil on panel

Lais of Corinth was a hetaira in ancient Greece who was famous for her dazzling beauty and her high price. The well-formed, elegantly proportioned beauty of the figure in the panel speaks for itself; the gold coins and the right hand stretched out towards the viewer draw attention to the payment the woman expects for her services. Whether the courtesan is to be equated with the Lais who sat for, and was the lover of, the most noted painter of antiquity, Apelles, is still a matter of speculation.

The worldly-wise elegance of pose and expression of this courtesan, combined with the soft and smoky modelling of her features, shows the influence of Venetian painting, which, by the 1520s, was already renowned (and sometimes attacked) for its air of opulent hedonism.

Lais - said to have been the mistress of the ancient Greek artist, Apelles - signifies Mercenary Love, it has been thought that a similarly posed figure in a smaller work entitled Venus and Cupid (also in Basel) might be a pendant to this, representing Pure Love. However, although Venetian artists were familiar with the theme of `Sacred and Profane Love' contrasted, as in Titian's great work of that title, no such conclusion seems possible in Holbein's case.

As Giorgione's Judith reveals, Holbein's sources were preeminently the sinuous, well-proportioned figures that Leonardo and Raphael had used for their Madonnas (as `perfect' women) but which had taken on other, less spiritual qualities once they reached Venice. Nevertheless, Holbein's adaptation seems to restore some of the earlier Renaissance innocence and Lais's demure expression belies her supposedly brazen costume. The artist shows greater interest in effectively foreshortening the figure's right arm than in presenting a character of easy virtue.

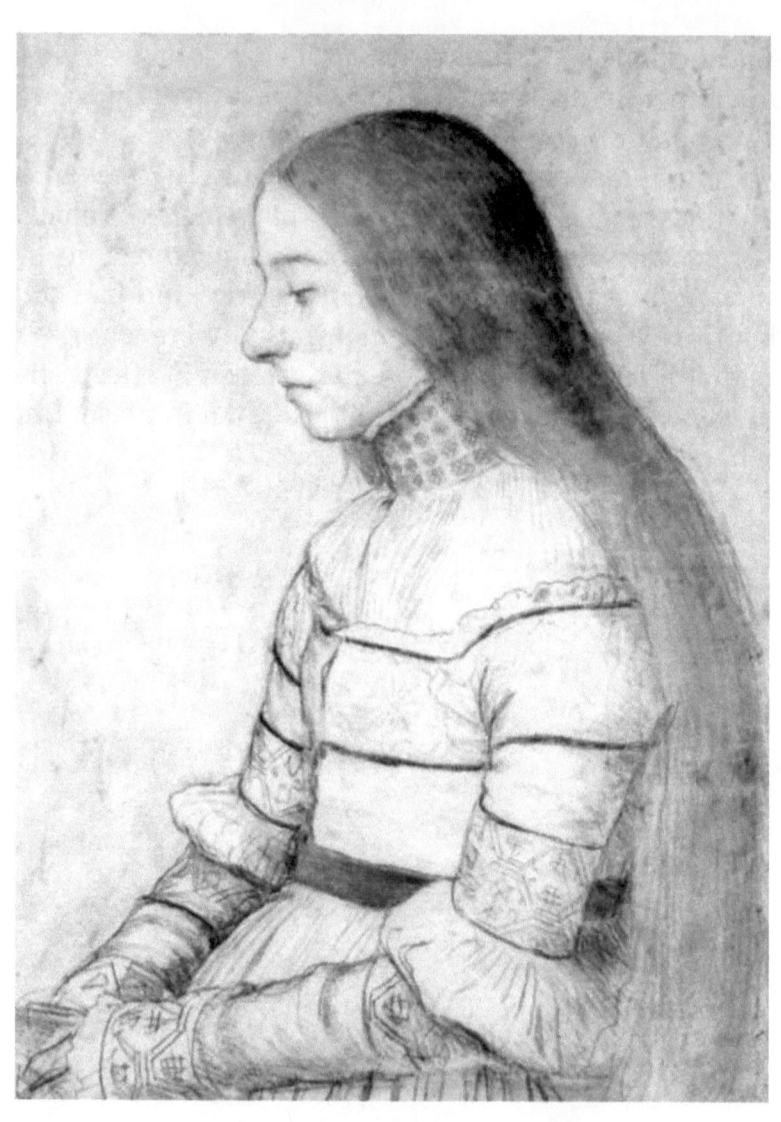

Portrait of Anna Meyer, c. 1526
Black and coloured chalks

This drawing was a preparatory study for the portrait of Anna Meyer in the Darmstadt Madonna. Here the sitter's hands, which in the painting hold a rosary, did not interest Holbein much as they are crossed out. Like the corresponding portrait drawings of Jakob Meyer and Dorothea Kannengiesser, this drawing also appears to have passed into the Meyers' possession, since in the 17th century all three apparently belonged to Remigius Faesch, a late descendant of Meyer's, with whose art collection they passed to the Kupferstichkabinett in Basel.

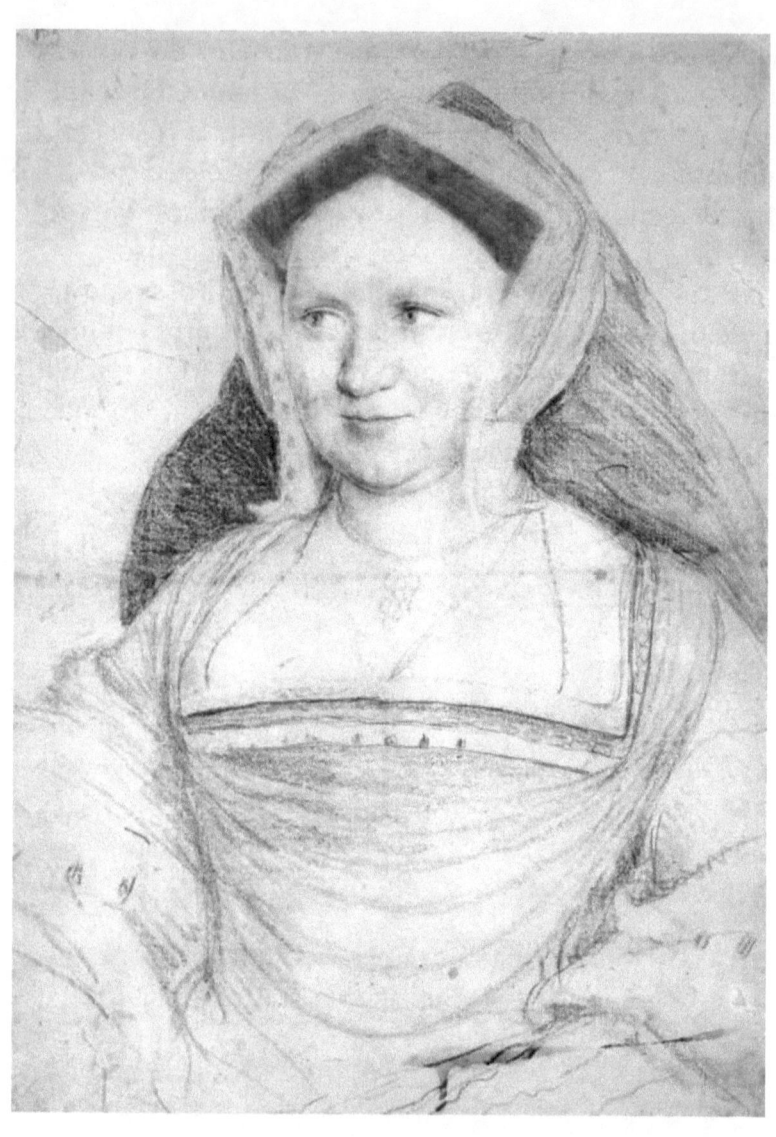

Portrait of Lady Mary Guildford, c. 1527
Black and coloured chalks

Unlike in the painting of Lady Mary Guildford, in this preparatory drawing her upper body and face are shown almost full frontally. However, she is looking to her right and the corners of her mouth are turned up slightly to produce an engaging expression. Except for these changes, the contours of the face in this study match exactly with those of the under-drawing of the painting. Holbein will thus have traced the outlines of the chalk drawing on to the panel. This is shown by the fact that individual lines, such as those of the nose, are strengthened on the drawing.

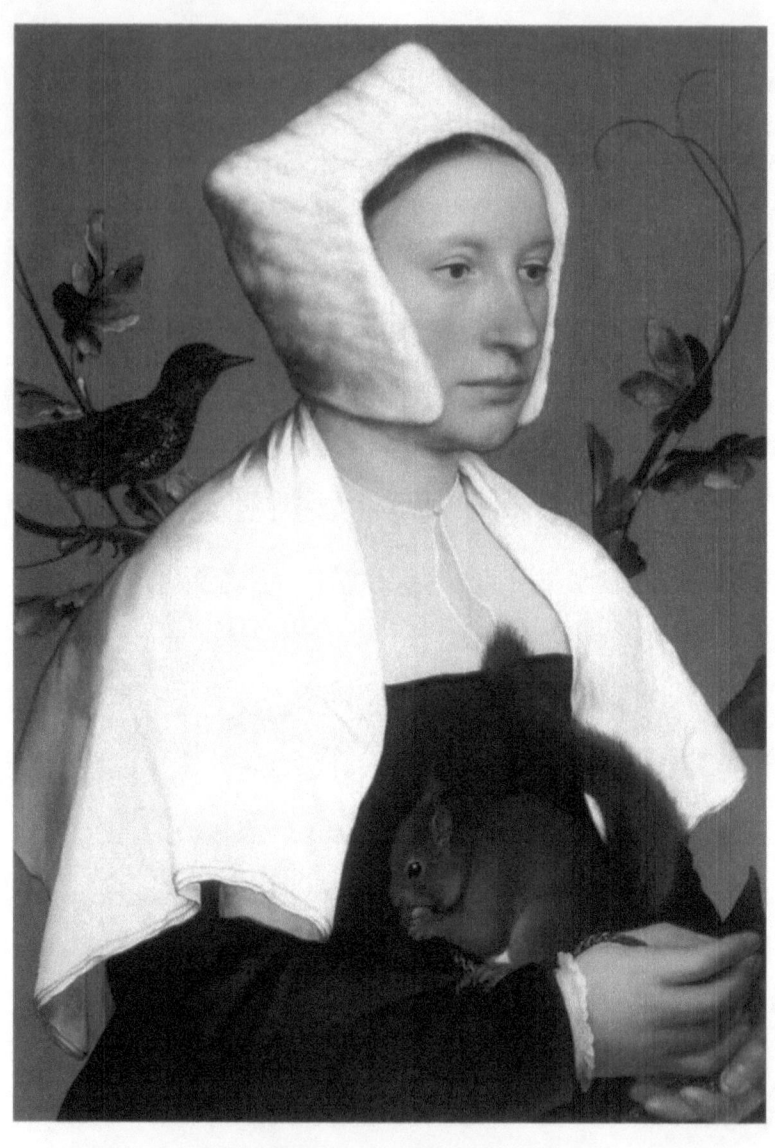

Lady with a Squirrel and a Starling, c.1527
Oil on panel

The portrait of a lady with a squirrel, a speckle-breasted starling perched behind her - perhaps as a pun on her name or a coat-of-arms brought to life - is a wonderfully preserved example of Holbein's art at its most evocative. The picture may have been painted as one of a pair depicting husband and wife. A vague resemblance between this woman and Margaret Giggs, who appears in the sketch of the More family, has often led to her being identified as the adopted daughter of Thomas More. In fact, the shared features are limited mainly to the comparable fur cap, which Margaret wears in an individual study in the royal collection at Windsor. Apparently the headgear corresponded with contemporary English fashion. On stylistic grounds, the picture can be dated to Holbein's first visit to England. In her warm fur cap the lady seems impassive, her eyes eluding the viewer's glance. Holbein's skill differentiates meticulously between the textures of the white fur, white shawl and the translucent white cambric buttoned at her throat and gathered in a ruffle at her wrist. The squirrel was added later over the sitter's clothes. Her hands, rearranged to support him, are a discordant note: they look masculine, modelled perhaps on those of an assistant in the studio. Yet the bright-eyed animal is essential to our reading of the portrait. His bushy tail, suggestively poised between the lady's gentle swelling breasts, hints at a sensuous nature beneath her reticently monochrome English costume.

This work demonstrates many of the features found in Holbein's work from his first English visit; the thoughtful, reserved expression of the sitter, less direct than in many later works, and the use of plant motifs to animate an otherwise flattened background. The lady's anonymity (she was most probably English and of the More circle, whose members were notably fond of animals) undoubtedly focuses attention on the meaning of the squirrel and starling's presence; these may have been intended as references to her name, or as living tokens of the family coat of arms. It is known that squirrels were often kept as pets at this time, while starlings are biddable companions. After the painting's recent cleaning, the squirrel's gleaming eye and soft fur have revealed Holbein to be as effective an animal painter as his German contemporary Hans Hoffman. Holbein's particular structural skill is evident in the way the squirrel's curling tail echoes the vine stem in the background, itself reminiscent of the Amerbach portrait.

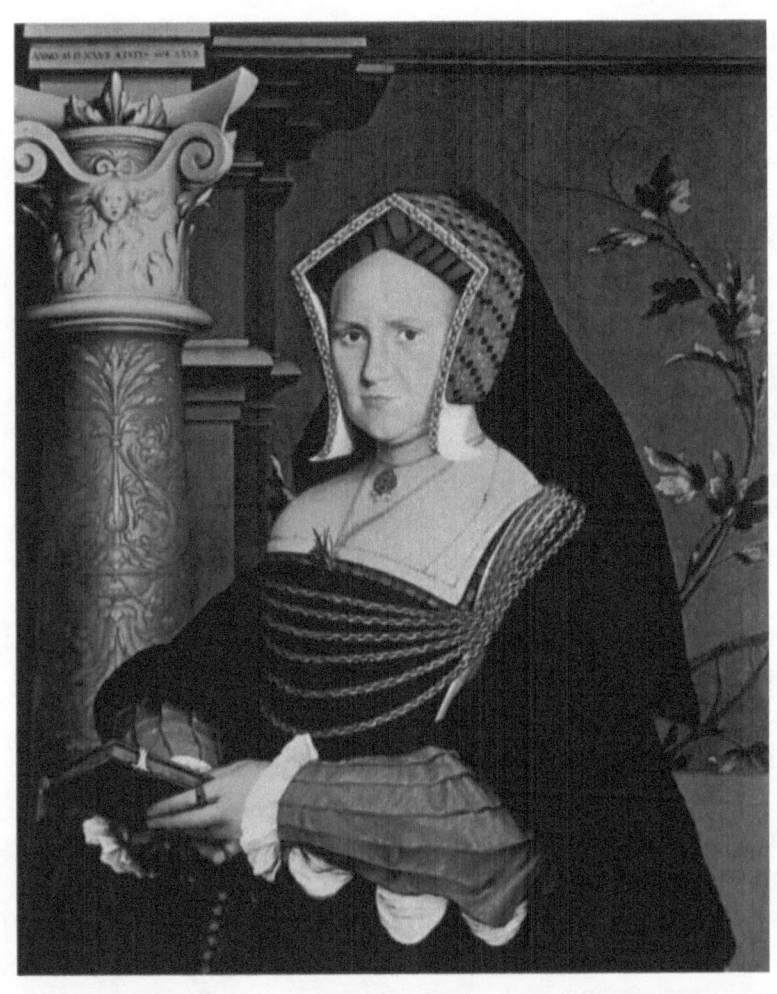

Portrait of Mary Wotton, Lady Guildenford, 1527
Tempera on wood

The second wife of Sir Henry Guildford, Mary Wotton had herself painted with a book of hours and a rosary. These attributes are formal references to a wife's piety, while the man is endowed with the attributes of worldly power. Although the panels are slightly different in size, they were conceived as a matching pair, as is indicated by the curtain pole that runs through both pictures and their matching blue backgrounds, decorated with the branches of vines. The preparatory drawing for this portrait is still held in Basel, which may indicate why the harsher lighting and greater linearity of the painting recalls Holbein's earlier European style. In comparison with the More family portraits, there is a stark flatness in the modelling of the plump sitter, whose figure is less comfortably integrated with the background. There is less interest in the texture of material (especially in the head dress), and awkward elements such as the grotesque head on the pillar seem to parody Lady Guildford herself. Holbein resorts to architectural as well as natural forms to rein in the composition, but despite the iron stanchion at the back and the receding perspectival column and pillars, ambiguities in space are unresolved at the far left and bottom right. Only the depiction of the sitter's arms and hands seems to have engaged the artist's full attention and powers.

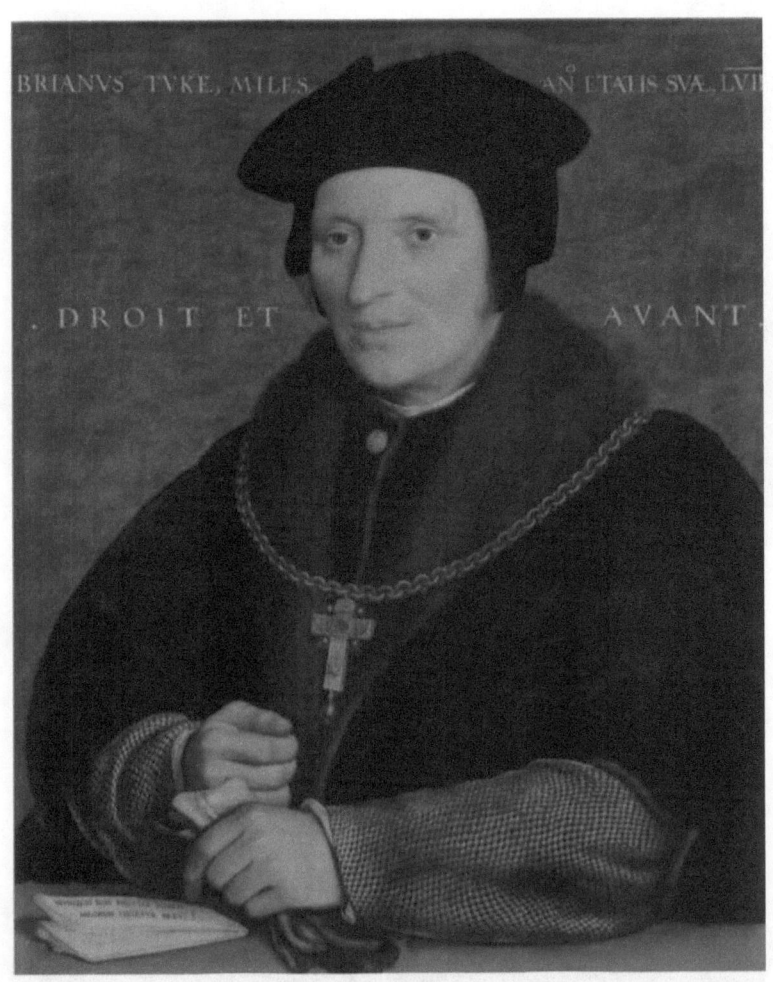

Portrait of Sir Brian Tuke, c.1527
Oil on wood

The dating is uncertain, some critics think it is a late
work from 1539-41. The folded paper with inscription,
and probably also the inscription in the background,
are later additions.

Several copies by the Holbein workshop, and some later copies exist, one in the Museum of Art in Cleveland, another in the Alte Pinakothek in Munich.

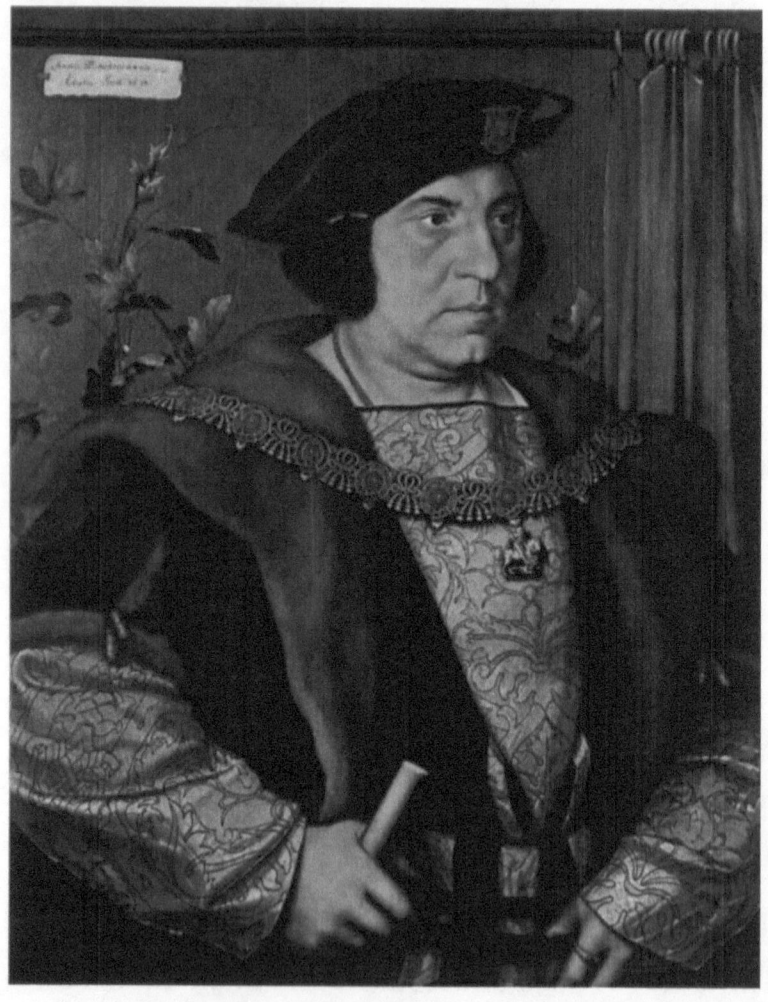

Portrait of Sir Henry Guildford, 1527
Oil on wood

Sir Henry Guildford (1489-1532), two years older than Henry VIII, was a great favourite of the King, ending his career at court as Comptroller of the Royal Household, whose baton of office he holds. He also wears the Order of the Garter, awarded him in 1526. Possibly the pictures of him and his wife were commissioned for this occasion, because the panels were completed the following year. (The dating is definite, as the matching portrait of Lady Guildford is dated to 1527.He was a strong proponent of religious reform.)

In comparison with the preparatory drawing held at Windsor, the sitter appears sterner and more conscious of office; worldly power emanates from his bulky figure, which swamps the background in the way Henry himself was also to do.

Sensitive though the modelling and shading of the face are, they reveal less empathy than is evident in the portrait of More. A trace of latent tension or paranoia, akin to that felt in Florentine Mannerist works gives an edgy quality to the apparently self assured form, enhanced by the brittle lighting at the top left of the picture which brings the vine and its tendrils into prominence. The badge on Guildford's cap bears geometrical forms which are also found in Durer's Melancolia I (1514).

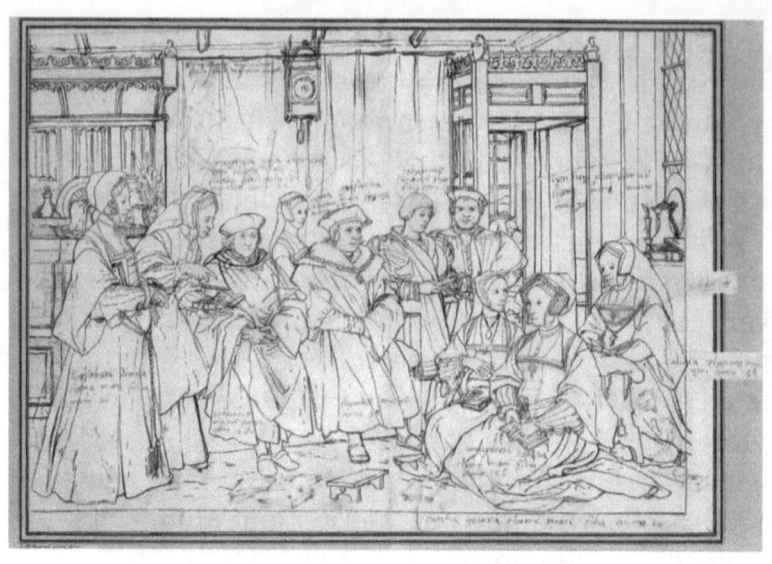

Study for the Family Portrait of Sir Thomas More, c. 1527
Pen and brush in black on top of chalk sketch

This is a preparatory study for the lost group portrait of the More family. The astronomer Nikolaus Kratzer (1487-1550), who taught in the More household, has noted in Latin besides the figures their names and ages. On the left is Elizabeth Dauncy (1506-1564), Thomas More's youngest daughter, while beside her is the adopted daughter Margaret Giggs (1508-1570) explaining a point of text to old Sir John More (c. 1451-1530). Thomas More sits grandly in the centre, with (left and right of him) the engaged couple Anne Cresacre (1512-1577) and young John More (c. 1509-1547), Thomas More's only son. Beside John More, and looking directly out of the picture, is the household fool, Henry Patenson. On the right of the picture are Cecily Heron, born 1507, and his eldest daughter, Margaret Roper, (1505-1544); his second wife, Lady Alice, kneeling at a prie-dieu, rounds off the picture on the right.

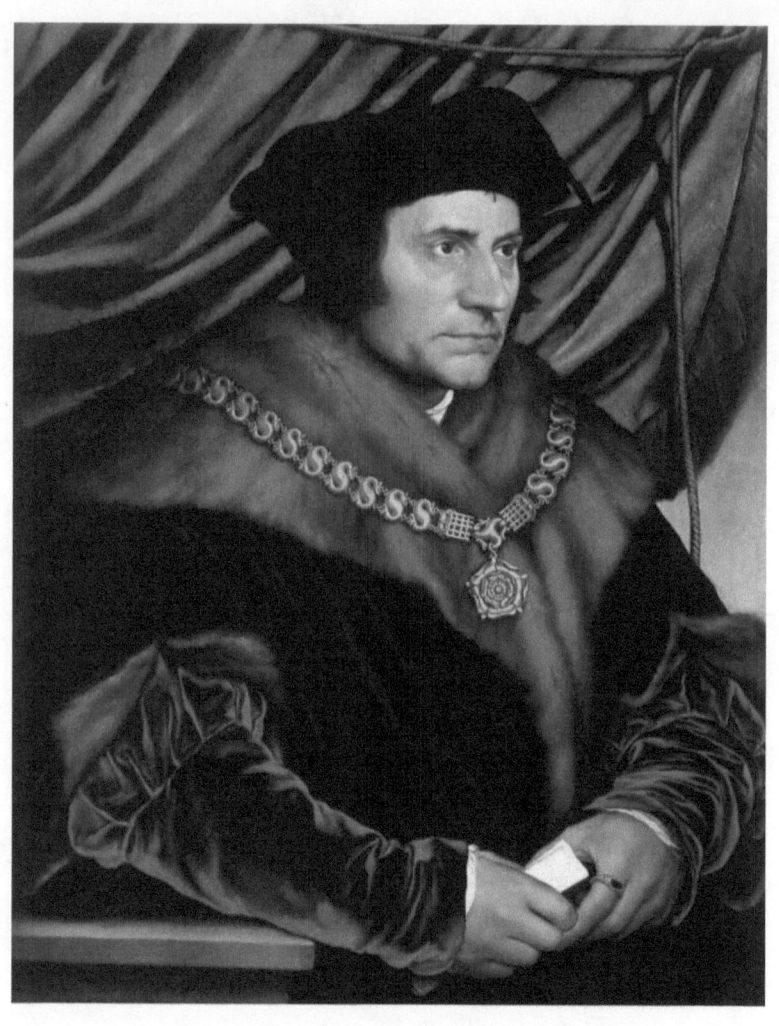

Portrait of Sir Thomas More, 1527
Oil on panel

Sir Thomas More (1477-1535) was humanist and statesman, chancellor of England (1529-32), who was beheaded for refusing to accept King Henry VIII as head of the Church of England. He is recognized as a saint by the Roman Catholic Church. He was the most important patron of Holbein during his first stay in London.

Along with Colet and Linacre, More was one of the moving spirits of the revival of learning and letters in the early years of Henry VIII's reign. The King himself seemed to presage a new civilized age and was keen to attract foreign artists and intellectuals to embellish his extrovert court; Erasmus himself was tempted to stay in England but finally refrained.

Holbein presents the public figure, robed in authority (for all his saintly reputation More was ferocious enough to condemn heretics to be burnt). The determined severity of countenance betrays little of the retiring scholar, although this is suggested in the figure's slight stoop. More was certainly concerned with the impression he made, insisting on having the flamboyant cuffs on his official costume replaced by ascetic plain ones.

When this portrait was painted in 1527, More held the office of Chancellor of the Duchy of Lancaster. He had been knighted in 1521. It is not known whether the golden chain of office made of S-shaped links was bestowed on him on this occasion or earlier, in 1517, when he first entered the king's service, the chain indicating the willing submission of the wearer. It is typical of Holbein's method that the half length figure composition repeats the tried-and-tested composition of the Venus and Lais pictures. The colours used in More's portrait, however, give the composition an entirely different mood.

The fine drawings made prior to the painting show a new delicacy of touch prevalent in the artist's manner after his visit to France; greater attention to the texture of material, fur and velvet was the painterly consequence. The emergence of complementary red and green tonalities to stress spatial values is apparent, but is more straightforward here than its usage in Holbein's second English period.

In the Royal Collection, Windsor, there is a preparatory drawing for this painting. Several copies of the painting exist in different collections. The copy in the Prado, Madrid, was made by Rubens during his stay in England in 1529/30.

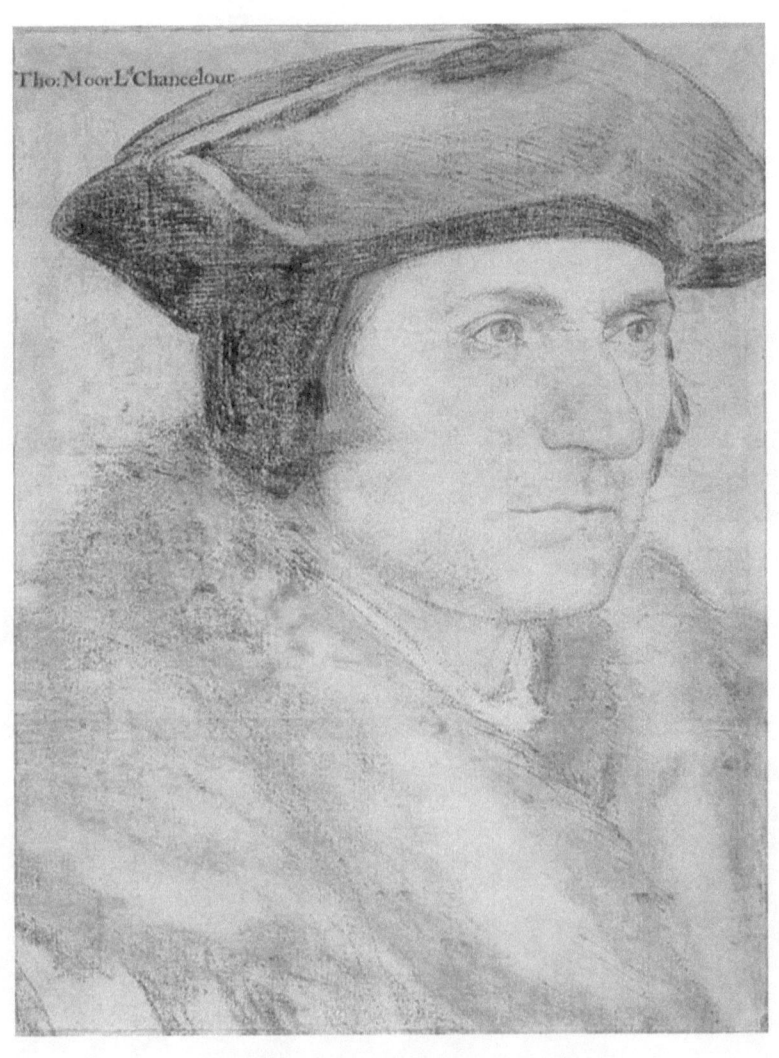

Sir Thomas More, 1527-28
Black and coloured chalks on paper

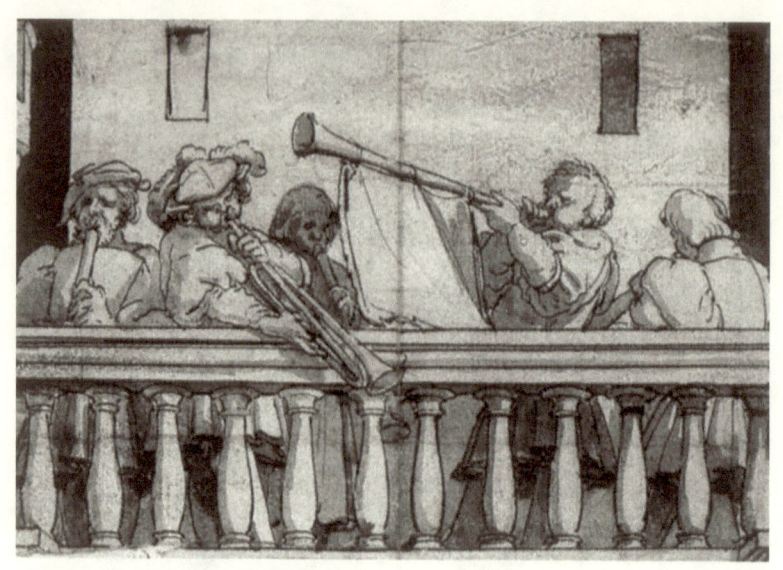

Musicians on a Balcony, c. 1527
Pen and black ink, with gray wash

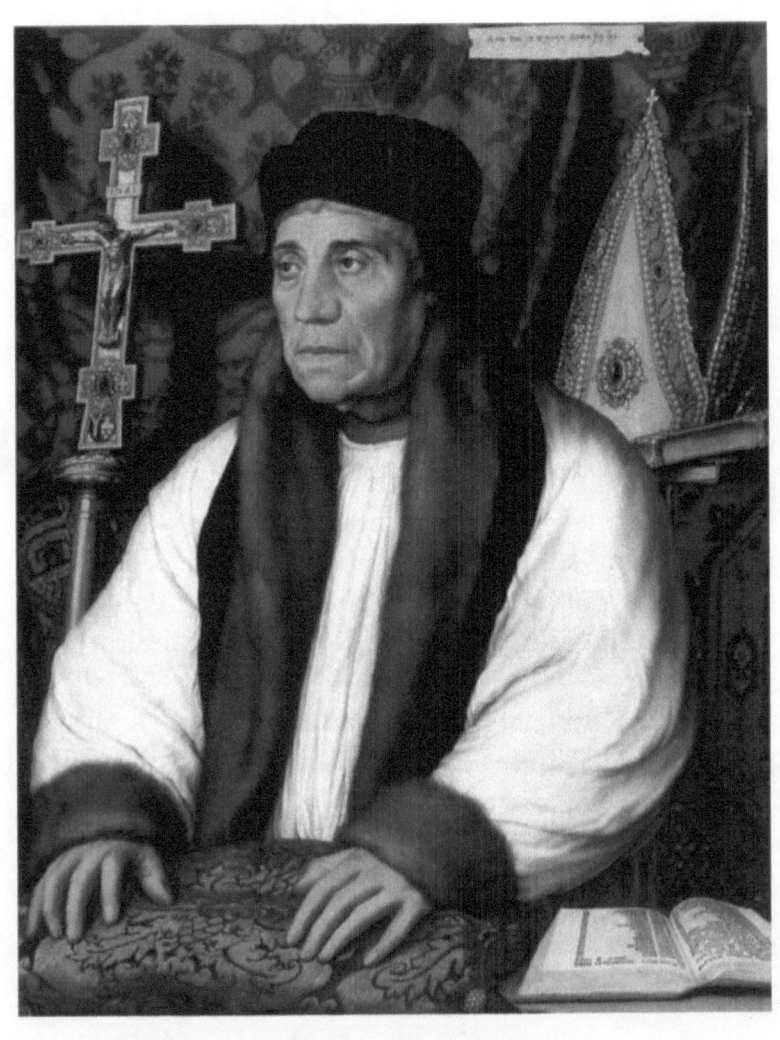

Portrait of William Warham, Archbishop of
Canberbury, 1527
Oil on panel

William Warham (1450-1532) was the last of the pre-Reformation archbishops of Canterbury, a quiet, retiring intellectual who nonetheless closed his career with a resolute stand against the anticlerical policies of King Henry VIII of England. Lord Chancellor from 1504 to 1515, William Warham was the man who crowned the young royal couple Henry VIII and Catherine of Aragon (1485-1536) in 1509. He remained faithful to the Roman Catholic Church all his life and when, after 1529, Parliament took more and more steps to restrict the authority of the Pope during the conflict over the King's divorce, the archbishop protested. Nonetheless, he died a natural death at a ripe old age in 1532, and unlike many others, like St Thomas Becket, the earlier archbishop whom he revered, did not have to pay with his life for his fidelity to the Catholic Church.

Whereas in The Solothurn Madonna the gold settings of the precious stones adorning the miter of St Nicholas are simulated with yellow paint, in this portrait of Warham, Holbein used real gold applied with a brush for rendering William Warham's episcopal miter. This is typical of his works in the period after his journey to France.

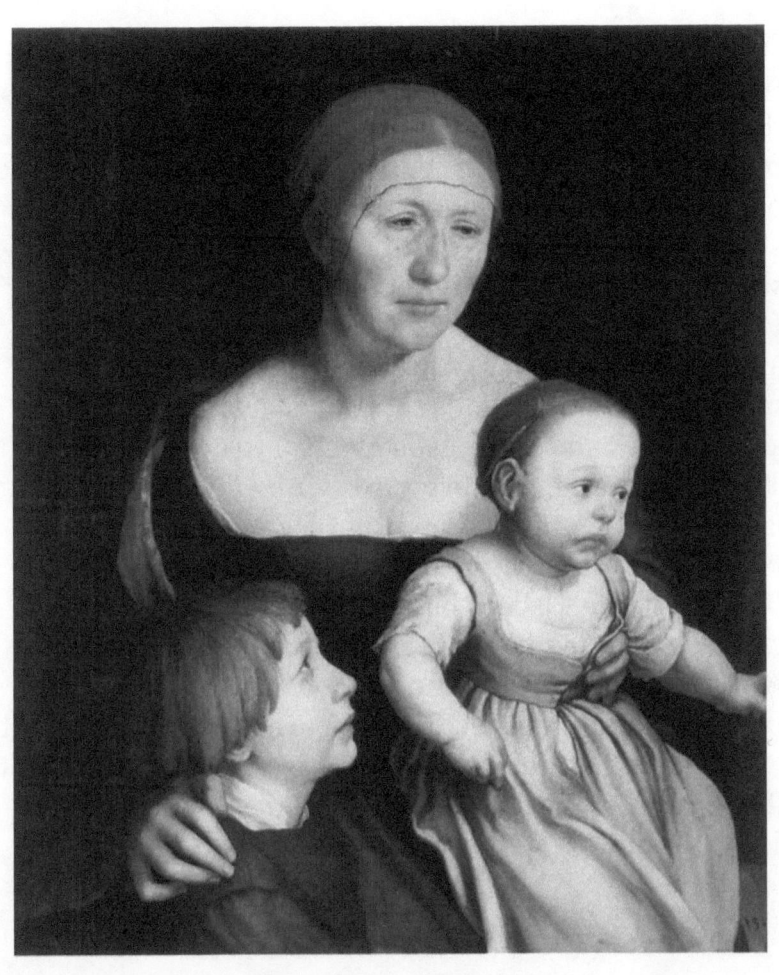

Charity (The Family of the Artist), c.1528
Oil on panel

Holbein dated this family portrait, which is painted on paper, in the bottom right-hand corner, but the last digit was lost when the figures were cut out round the outline later in the 16th century and subsequently stuck on a black-painted panel. Several considerations strongly suggest the portrait must date from 1528, shortly after Holbein's return from England: his son Philipp, born around 1522, is about six in the picture, and his daughter Katharina is hardly more than two; moreover, his children Jakob and Kьngold, born around 1529 and 1530 respectively, are not present. The identification of the figures with Holbein's family is based on an entry in the Amerbach inventory produced in 1587 asserting that the portrait is of Holbein's wife Elsbeth Binzenstock and his two eldest children, painted in oil on paper and mounted on wood. When Holbein returned to England, he left the picture behind in Basel. Elsbeth parted with the portrait even before her husband's death, as by 1542 at the latest it belonged to the Zurich painter Hans Asper (1499-1571). Basilius Amerbach acquired it in 1579.

The moving combination of resolution and frailty seen in this family portrait is unique in Holbein's production. The introverted mood of the work extends beyond the usual level of reticence in his English portraits, where courtly finery and the dignity inherent in status to some extent shield the private lives of the sitters. The work provokes consideration of the relationship between the painter and his wife, who was separated from him for years at a time, bringing up their four children alone. The strain of this fractured family life may be seen here in the weary resignation of Elsbeth's wan face. The sober colours and emphasis on linear execution (seen in young Philip's profile) are perhaps concessions to what was acceptable in reformist Basel at the time, although elements of the dislocated triangle of the composition and the modelling of the mother's hand on the boy's shoulder are reminiscent of Leonardo's The Virgin and Child with Saint Anne, which Holbein probably saw during his visit to France in 1524.

The painting's dour background is a later result of cutting out the figures and laying them down on a panel; originally, there may well have been a decorative background as is the case in one copy.

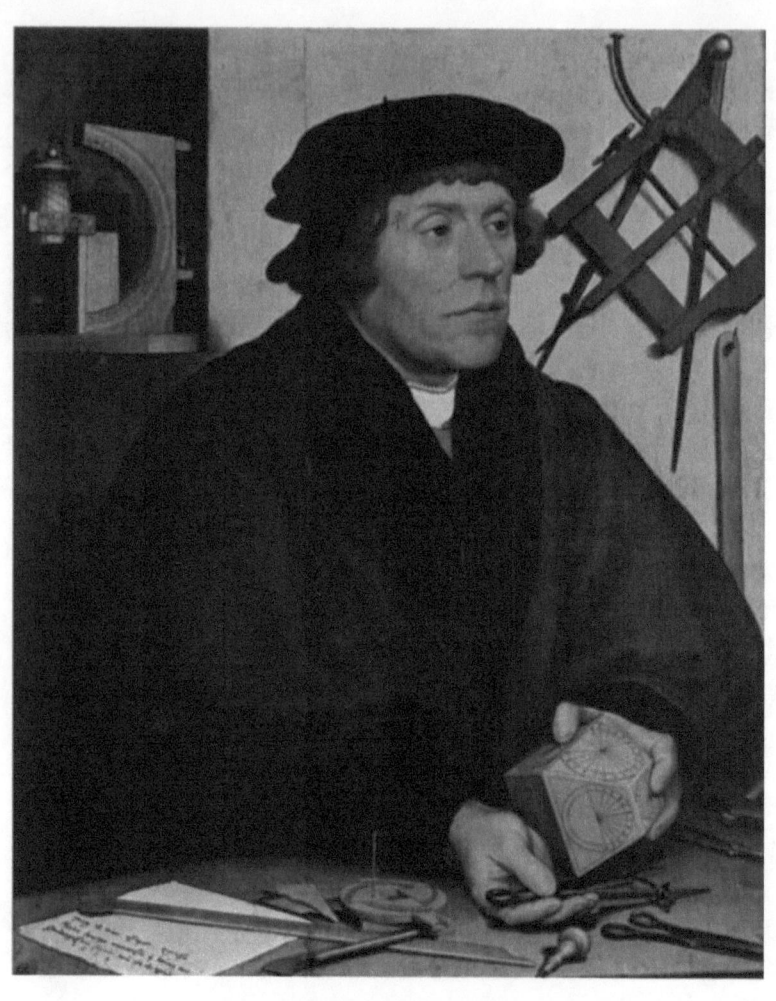

Portrait of Nicholas Kratzer, 1528
Oil on panel

Kratzer (1487 - c.1550) was born in Munich and studied in Cologne and Wittenberg. From a letter sent by Petrus Aegidius to Erasmus on January 19, 1517, we know that "Nicolaus Bavarus" was due to travel from Antwerp to Brussels to sell astronomical equipment. In the same year, Kratzer was appointed professor in Corpus Christi College, Oxford, and henceforth remained in England. A humanist, he was a close friend of Thomas More and from 1519 the royal court astronomer in the service of Henry VIII. He was employed by both More and Cardinal Wolsey (whose downfall occurred a year after the portrait was painted).

The painting is pivotal in many respects. Despite being a product of his first stay in England, Holbein developed the allusive style of illustrating his sitter's career (as a maker of mathematical and geometrical instruments) to new levels of coherence. Although a display of similar items was to recur in The Ambassadors, there they are passive witnesses of mental concerns, while the refreshing directness of Kratzer's practical involvement means that his character is not buried by the artist's determination to include convincing still-lives.

Compared with the Guildford portraits, a new mastery is evident, in the subtlety of lighting, the elegant range of cream, brown and black tones in the pattern of instruments against the wall, and in the presentation of Kratzer's idiosyncratic heavy-lidded gaze. It is revealing to contrast this humane mood with the archly aristocratic tone of Bronzino's Ugo Martelli.

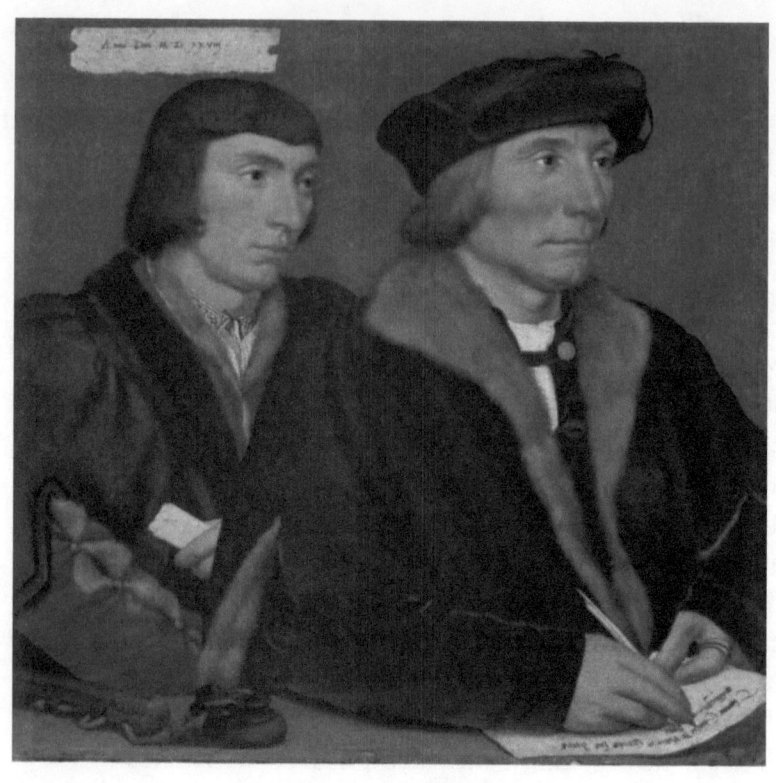

Double Portrait of Sir Thomas Godsalve and His Son
John, 1528
Resin tempera on oak

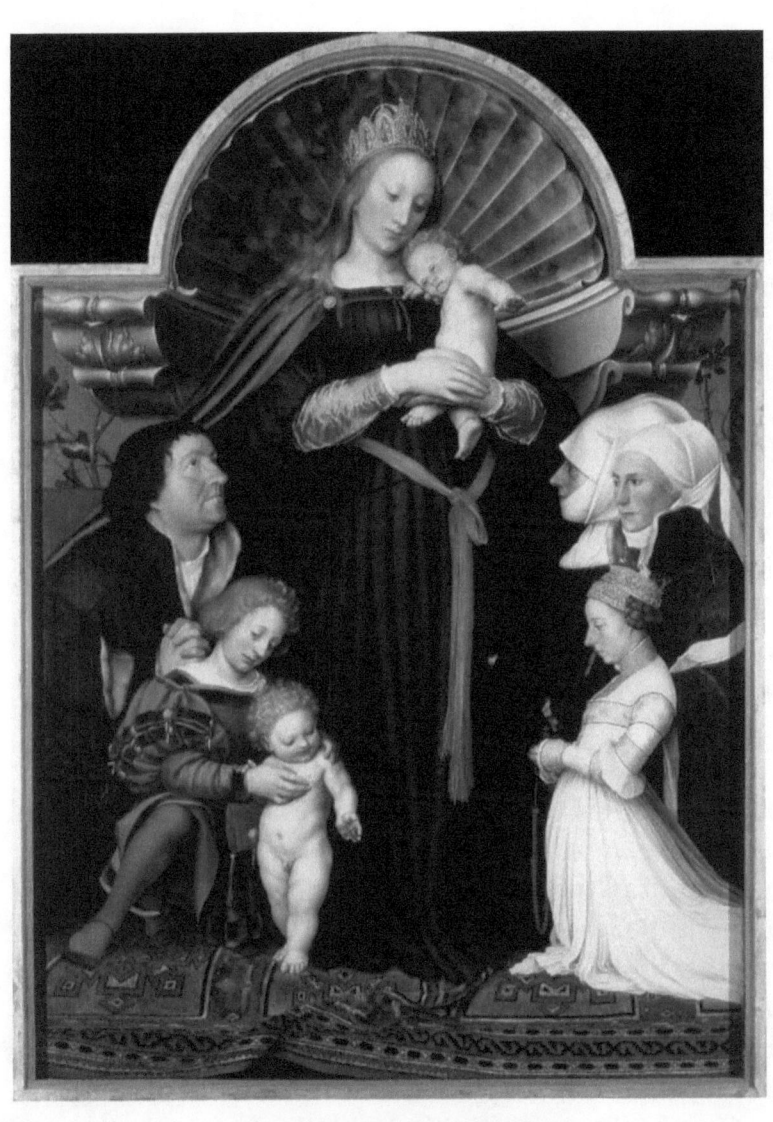

Darmstadt Madonna, 1528
Oil on limewood

The Meyer or Darmstadt Madonna is the last, most famous and most effective of Holbein's great religious works, above all in its depiction of individual human identities combined with spectacular spatial control and illusionism - as exemplified by the ruckled carpet. Standing in a scalloped niche with projecting consoles, Mary, with the Christ Child in her arms, is surrounded by the Meyer family. The hooped crown, an allusion to the German imperial crown, identifies her as the Queen of Heaven. Typologically, the painting is a Schutzmantelbild (a `Virgin of Pity' painting), in which the donor, Jakob Meyer, invokes and gains divine protection for himself and his family. Unusually, the donor is shown as the same size as the Virgin. Chastened by worldly failure and disgrace, Meyer no longer staunchly outstares the world but has his eyes fixed on other realms in meditative intensity. This introspection is echoed by his wives the enigmatic enwrapped profile of his first, Magdalena Baer (who had died in 1511) and Dorothea Kannengiesser. Before them kneels Anna, the only surviving child, whose portrait drawing in chalk shows her with free-flowing hair. Holbein repainted her hair tied in a band after her engagement.

In front of Jakob, in a Raphaelesque triangular pose deployed with subtlety and skill, his two deceased sons are depicted. The baby, with curly blonde hair and pudgy cheeks, has affinities with the Leonardo type. Also Leonardesque is the prowess shown in the foreshortening of the Christ-child's extended arm, and the naturalness of the baby's pose, which recall The Virgin of the Rocks.

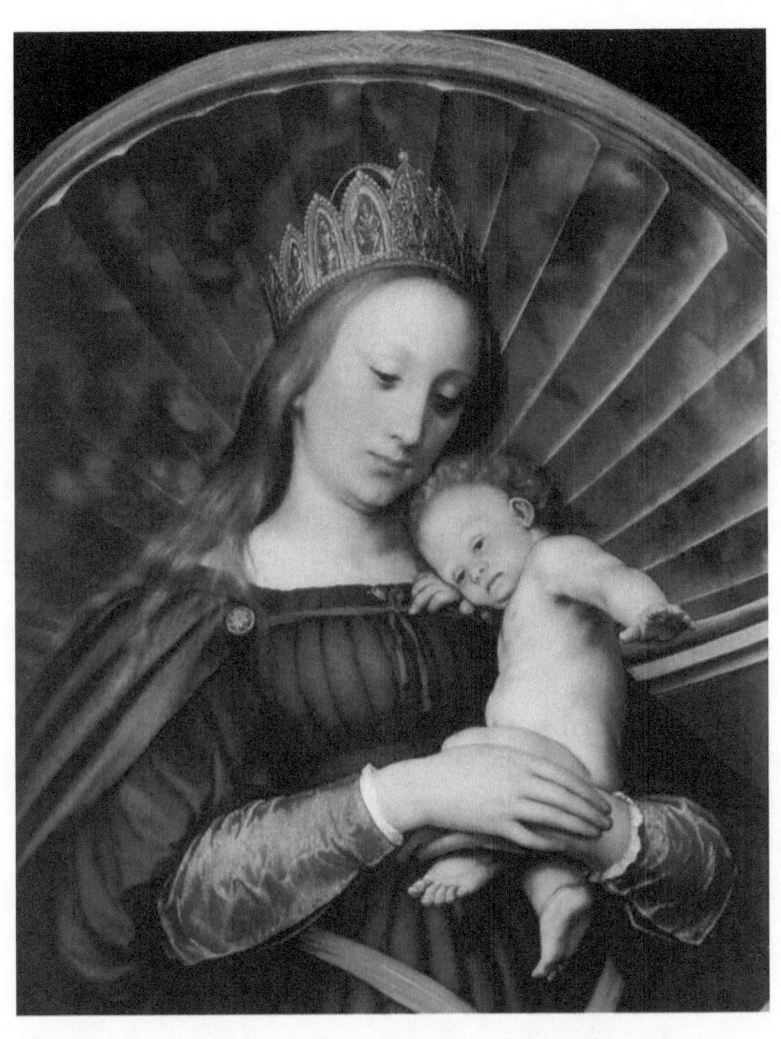

Darmstadt Madonna (detail)

The presentation of the Madonna and Child is a triumph of illusionism that ranks with the achievements of Van Eyck in Flanders a century before. The play of light over the fluting of the architectural shell behind the two figures carves out the space into which the delicately shadowed crown, hair and face of the Madonna are set. There is no Raphaelesque regularity in the Madonna's features - as with most northern Madonnas, a specific model was used, a friend of Holbein's, one Magdalena Offenburg who also posed for the Lais and whose lifestyle, ironically, was not considered blameless.

However, the compelling physical presence and credibility of the figures is the result of artistic means alone; the twisting of the child's body emphasizes the weight the Madonna's arms must carry, and Christ's projecting feet and the foreshortening of his own and his mother's arms stress the space his torso occupies. The combination of warm green and gold also brings the Madonna forward against the neutral .tone of the stonework.

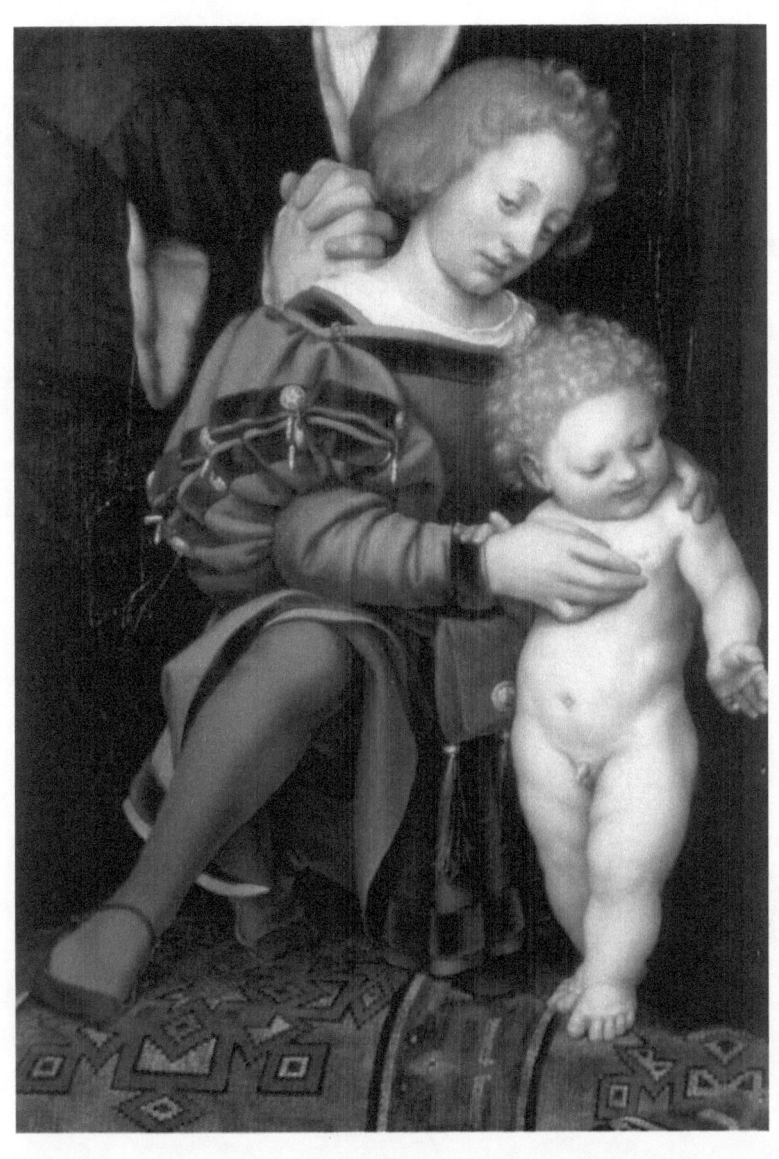

Darmstadt Madonna (detail)

Unlike Anna Meyer, the figures of the boys are not portraits, since they lack any individual features. In his elegant face and hands, the squatting youth bears striking resemblance to the Mary figure, which, in contrast to the Solothurn Madonna, is idealized in the manner of the Raphael model. The naked boy and the Child Jesus also correspond to figure types found in Italian Renaissance paintings, and it is conceivable that Holbein was inspired by compositions by Raphael and Leonardo that he had seen on his trip to France.

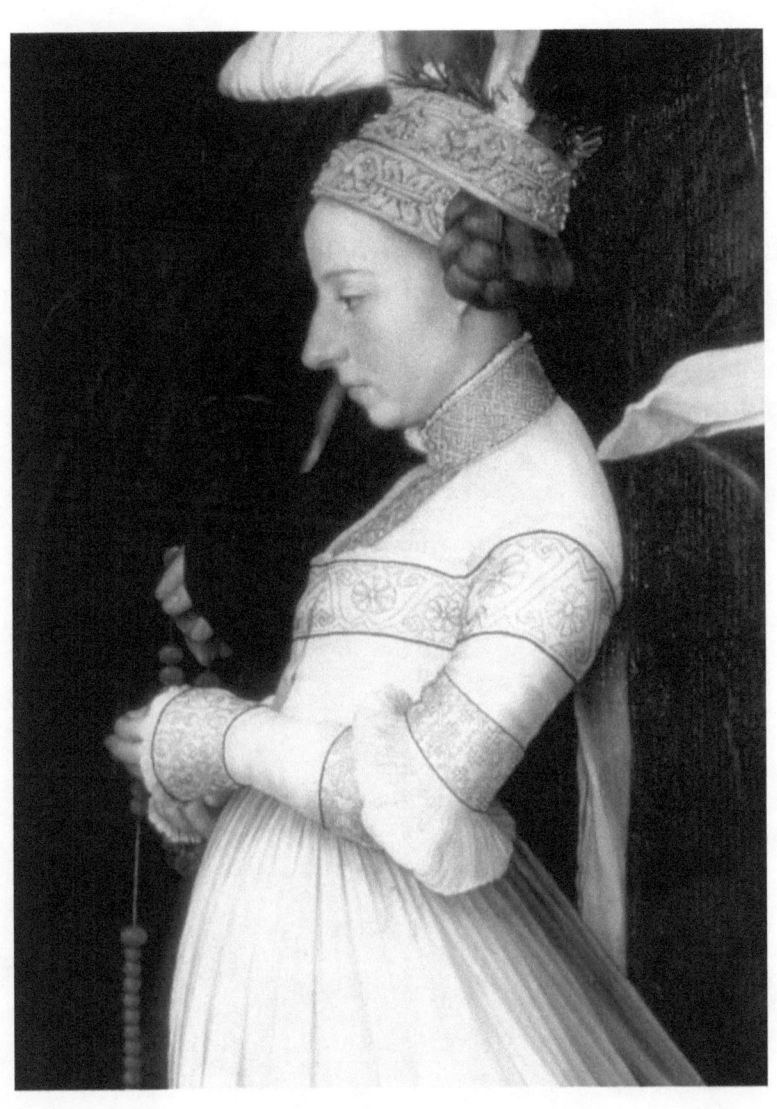

Darmstadt Madonna (detail)

In the portrait study, Anna Meyer is shown seated, whereas here she is kneeling. In the drawing she cannot be older than 13-15, and given that the parents were married in 1513, Holbein must have been given the commission for the Madonna panel before he left for England in 1526. On his return, he revised the picture, putting Anna's hair up and tucking most of it under her chaplet. Smaller changes were made to the outline of her face, particularly to make the girl look somewhat older.

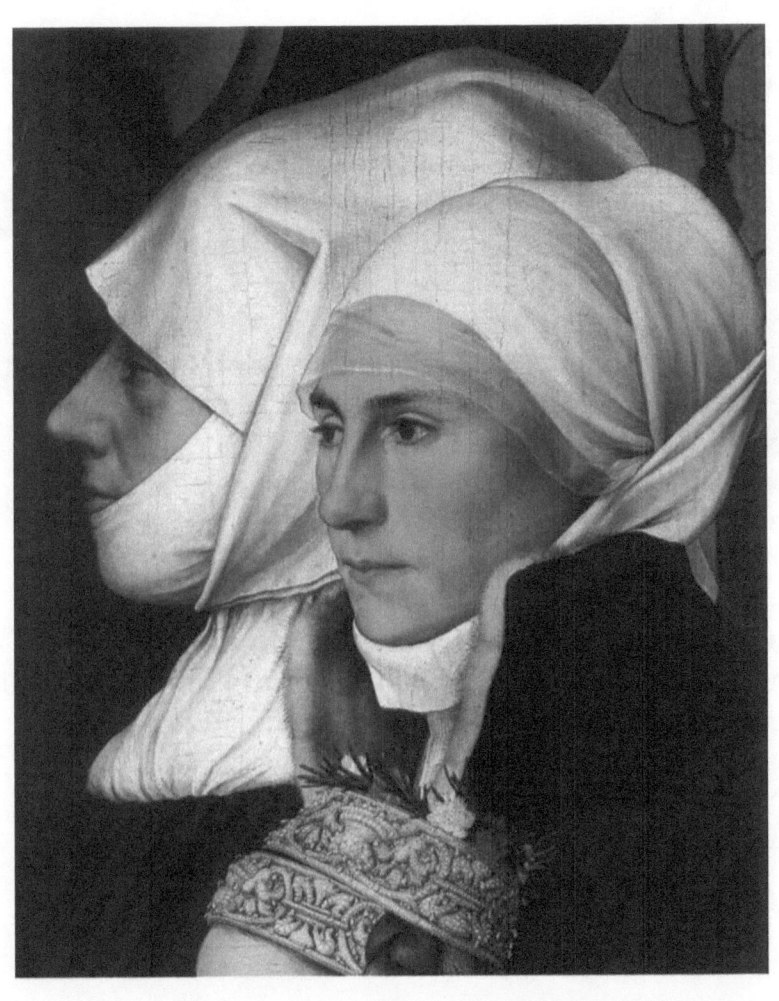

Darmstadt Madonna (detail)

Jakob Meyer's unusual stipulation that the artist include his deceased first wife Magdalene in the painting was the result of the death of Meyer's two sons during Holbein's first English absence: he decided to include all members of his family, living and dead, rather than omit any individual. Holbein brilliantly resolved the problem of tactfully integrating Magdalena's portrait into the group. The use of the profile and her retiring position at the back avoid direct eye contact, and the swathing of her face in cloth ensures that her features - which Holbein had never seen - do not seem vapid in comparison to the forceful portrayals of the rest of the family.

The great skill and delicacy of the detailing of Anna's hair-band, catching the translucent light over the pearls, recalls the attention to detail of the old Flemish masters and their early explorations of the powers of oil paint. In this private work for the Meyer chapel at Gross Gundeldingen Holbein achieved a combination of piety and grandeur, and interaction between the human and divine, to rival that of Van Eyck himself.

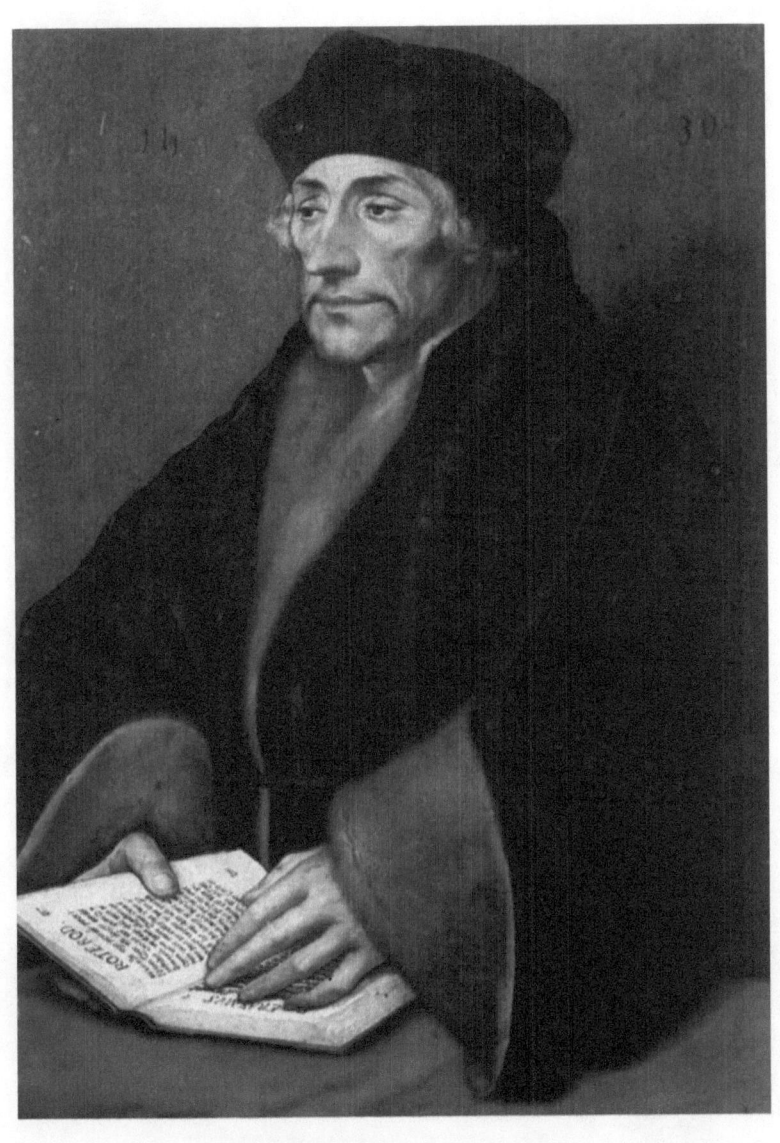

Portrait of Erasmus of Rotterdam, 1530
Oil on wood,

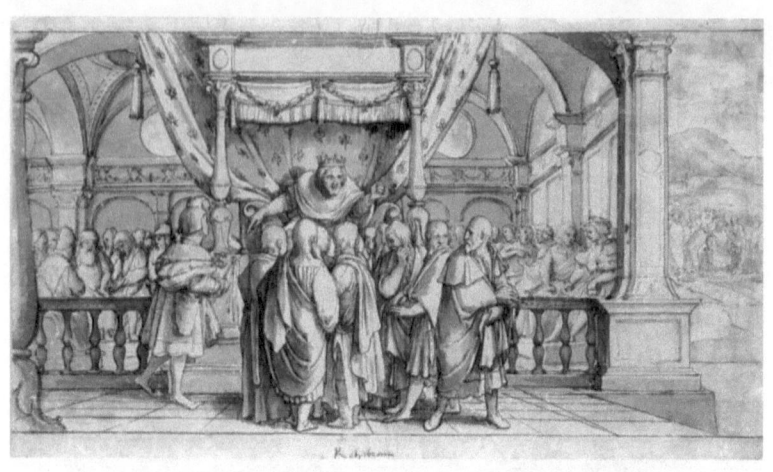

The Arrogance of Rehoboam, c. 1530
Pen and brown ink and chalk, tinted with gray wash
and watercolour

For the paintings on the south wall of the Great Council
Chamber, a program of Old Testament scenes was
chosen, possibly as a reaction to the Reformation,
which took root in Basel in 1529. The scene with
Rehoboam provided the Council with the example of a
bad ruler: Rehoboam, son of the wise king Solomon,
drove the tribes of Israel to break with the House of
David by refusing to moderate his excessively harsh
regime.

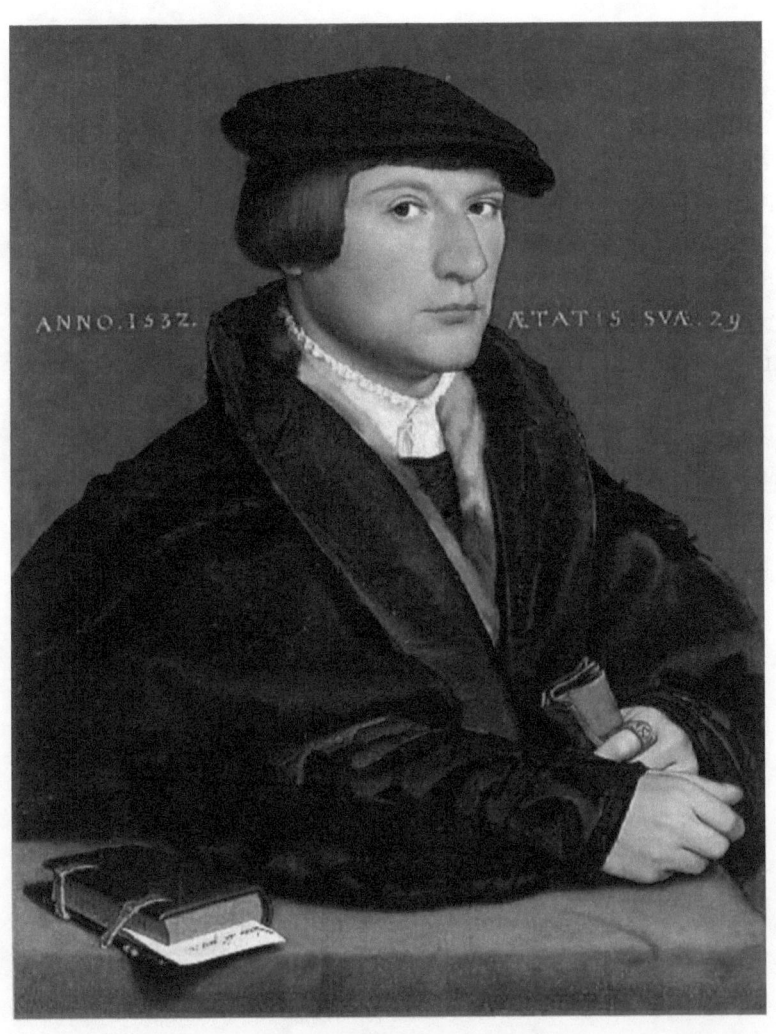

Portrait of a Member of the Wedigh Family, 1532
Oil on panel

Hans Holbein was a true Renaissance man. Equally at home in Basel and London, he was a friend of the great humanists of his day and produced works ranging from paintings to book illustration to designs for stained glass. This picture demonstrates why Holbein is regarded as one of the world's greatest portraitists. The clarity of colour, the precision of drawing, and the crisp, explicit characterization constitute a compelling likeness of an individual person. The sitter is a member of a Cologne trading family; presumably he was their representative in England, where Holbein found many clients among a wealthy community of German merchants who belonged to the Hanseatic League.

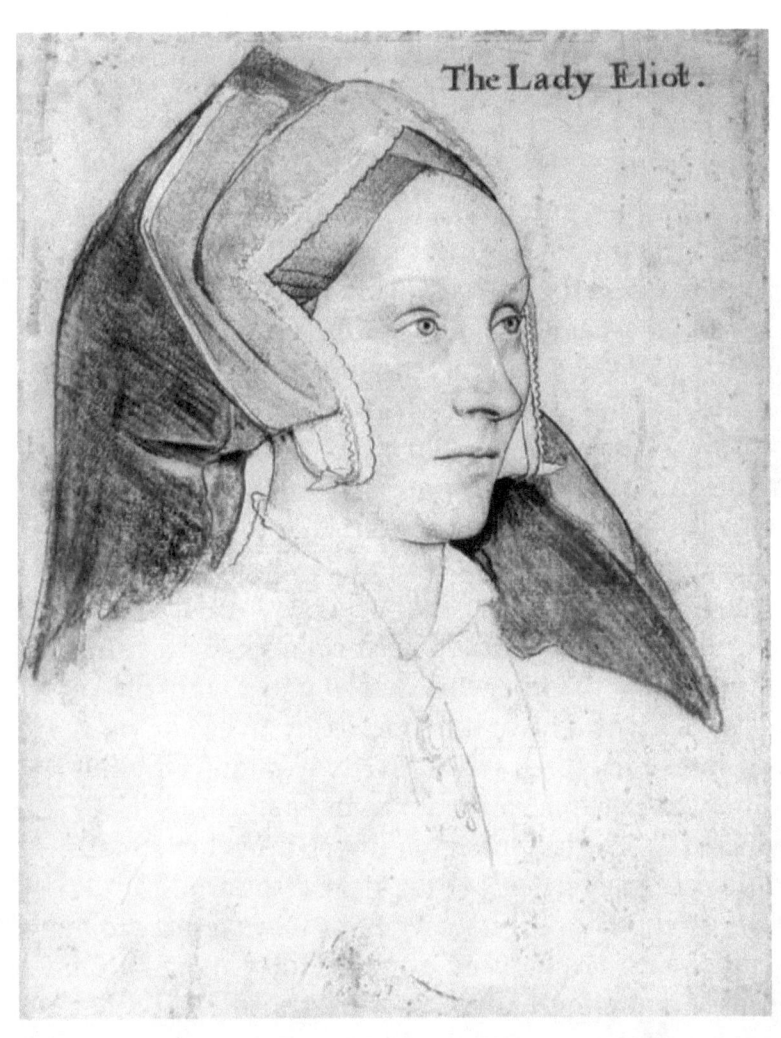

The Lady Eliot.

Lady Elyot, 1532-33
Chalk, pen and brush on paper

Although contemporaneous with such portraits as that of Gisze, this pair of portrait drawings (with Sir Thomas Elyot) nevertheless had a different goal. The examination of intellectual or ideological stance or status was not much sought after by the subjects of most of the English court and society portrayals Holbein undertook. That was more the domain of his German merchants and scientists. The pragmatic accuracy of `warts and all' delineation was what fascinated the English clients most, and such interest in detail can be traced back to the national traits in medieval manuscript illumination, where natural forms rather than abstract or geometrical patterns abound. Sometimes, the sitters were happy enough with Holbein's preparatory chalk drawing, and finished paintings did not ensue. There are no known paintings connected with either this drawing or that of Sir Thomas Elyot. The native perplexity over perspective and foreshortening, which partly explains why the miniature became so favoured in later Tudor times (since it precludes much of either), must have made Holbein's mastery of both appear astounding.

The starchy headdress Lady Eliot wears seems to have been of a design baffling even to Holbein (he had had trouble depicting Lady Guildford's in 1527), probably because of the way in which it prevents that definition of the back of the head which allows the face to jut into the picture space convincingly.

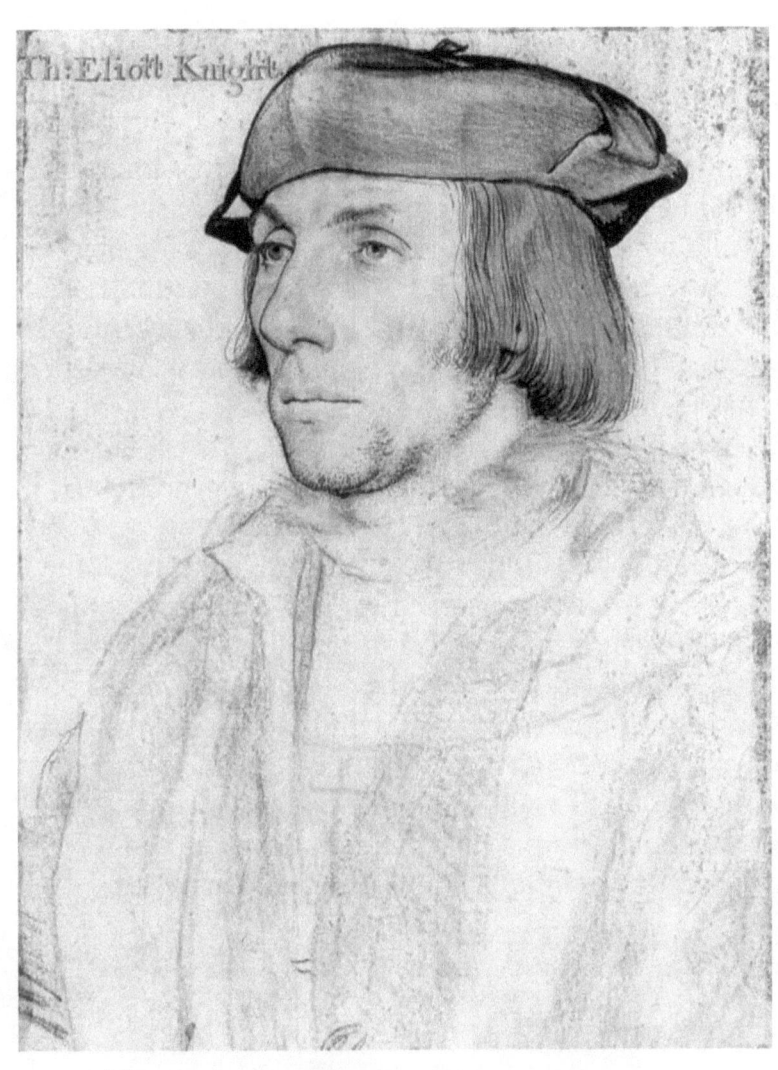

Sir Thomas Elyot, 1532-33
Chalk, pen and brush on paper,

Here, the flat hat and the falling hair give the head greater solidity, accentuated, as in the companion-piece, by the vaporous quality of the upper body. The striking use of black and yellow in each case sharpens the pink coloration of the prepared paper (useful for rendering flesh tones), and makes the drawing more forceful. As in earlier portrait drawings and the 1527 portrait of More, stubble on the man's chin accentuates sense of `here-and-now', the living presence marvelled at in the inscription on Derich Born portrait's.

Elyot was a member of Sir Thomas More's circle and praised him in `the boke named the Governour', his great treatise on education (1531). After More's execution however, he reneged, asking Cromwell to forget this ertswhile friendship. The Gouvernor was to wield influence up to and throughout Elizabeth I's reign, with its advocacy of the complete training a Renaissance mind and body would need, not restricted to narrow, academic learning alone. The book is thought to have been instrumental in determining the reformers to set up a tier of academies - the King Edward VI grammar schools - in the early 1550s.

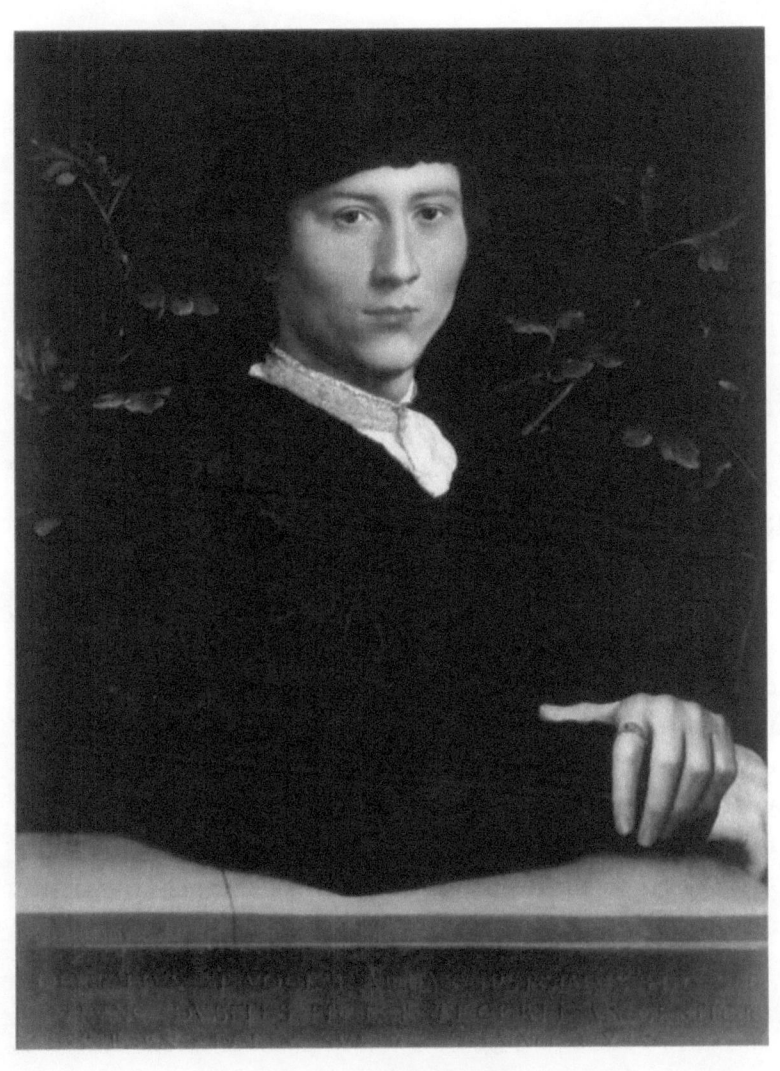

Portrait of Derich Born, 1533
Oil on wood

Hans Holbein the Younger returned to England in 1532 for a second and longer visit, marked by a series of portraits of German merchants in London's Steelyard community. The group formed part of the powerful Hanseatic League and its members were for the most part only based in London for a few years. Holbein painted the portraits of several merchants, not, as might well be assumed, for the decoration of the Steelyard Merchants' Hall, but most probably for their families left behind in Germany. (The success of these portraits, however, led the Steelyard Merchants to commission the allegorical paintings The Triumph of Riches and The Triumph of Poverty for their Hall.) The portraits are restricted to half-length compositions and the sitters are normally posed in relation to a parapet or a table, looking directly out at the viewer and often identified by an inscription or some other internal clue. In this context the present inscription is of a type often found on portraits during the Renaissance. The wording might indicate an informal purpose for the painting. Although the exact number of the Steelyard portraits is not known, seven of the sitters can be firmly identified.

When seen in sequence the paintings reveal the development of Holbein's portraiture during the early 1530s, from the meticulous treatment of the still-life objects in Portrait of George Gisze (Berlin, Gemäldegalerie) to the more restrained composition of the present portrait. Here the barrier formed by the parapet is negated by the placing of the head in relation to the angle of the shoulders and by the sitter's jutting elbow. These devices help to define the position of the figure both within the picture space and with regard to the viewer. They can also be found in early portraits by Titian such as the Portrait of a Man (also in the Royal Collection) and in the Portrait of Baldassare Castiglione by Raphael (Paris, Louvre). The precision of Holbein's brushwork incorporating the smooth modulation of the flesh tones, enhanced by the sharp light, the embroidery on the collar, and the foliage behind is remarkable. It has been suggested that the fig leaves behind the sitter in the present portrait are included for prophylactic reasons as opposed to being a personal symbol.

Derich Born was from Cologne and his mercantile activities are recorded between 1533, when he may already have been in England, and 1549. In 1536 he is documented as a supplier of harnesses at the time of the suppression of the Pilgrimage of Grace. Together with his brother, Johannes, Born was expelled from the London Steelyard in 1541 and he seems frequently to have been in financial difficulties even though he continued trading.

The portrait has the brand of Charles I on the back, but it seems not to have been recorded in any of the inventories of the Royal Collection until the reign of Charles II. It may, however, be identifiable with a portrait of Derich Born recorded in 1655 as being in the collection of Thomas Howard, Earl of Arundel, a great admirer of Northern European painting. Charles I often gave paintings to Howard or exchanged pictures with him. This seems, therefore, to be a case of a picture having left the Royal Collection only to return later.

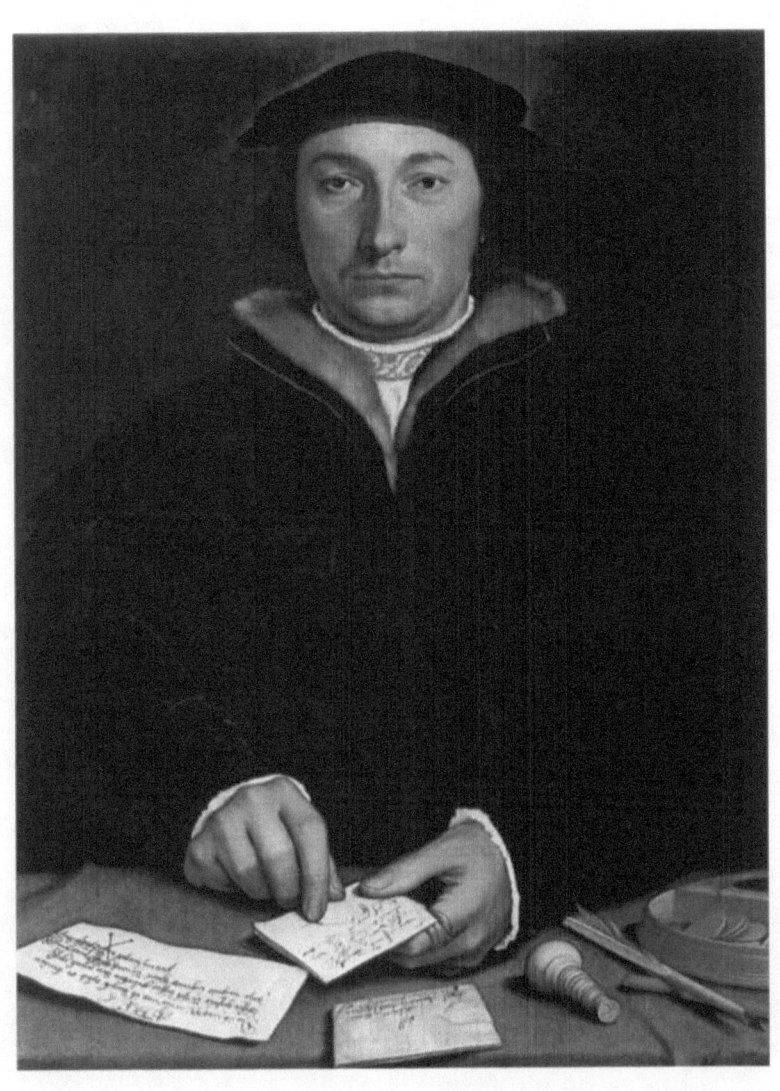

Portrait of Dirk Tybis, 1533
Oil on wood

In 1533, Dirk Tybis, then 33 and originally from Duisburg, was resident in London: we are told this on a piece of paper on the left on the table, which according to the inscription is in his own hand. The merchant's trademark is inscribed between his first and family names. The letter Tybis points to with his right index finger is addressed to him, and his initials appear also on the third document.

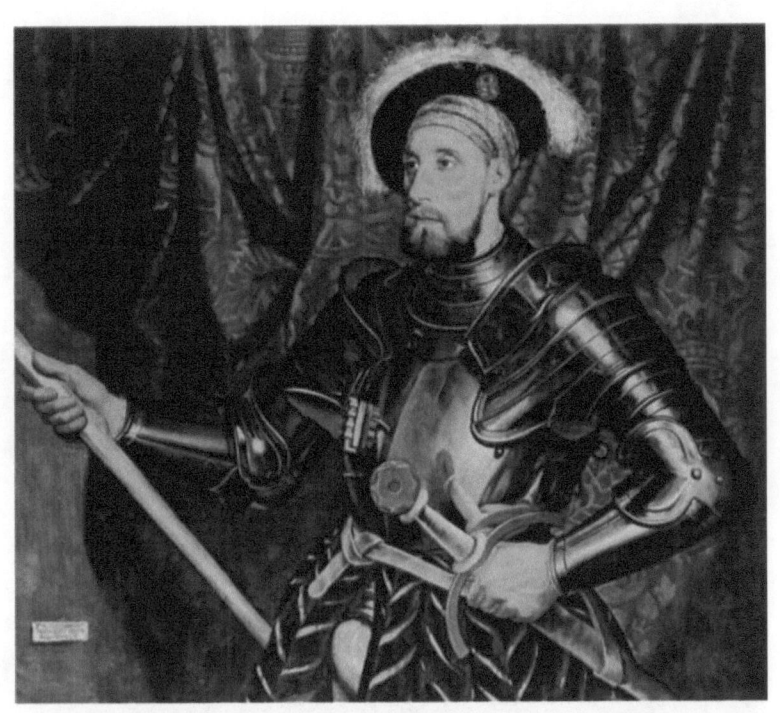

Portrait of Sir Nicholas Carew, c.1533
Tempera on wood

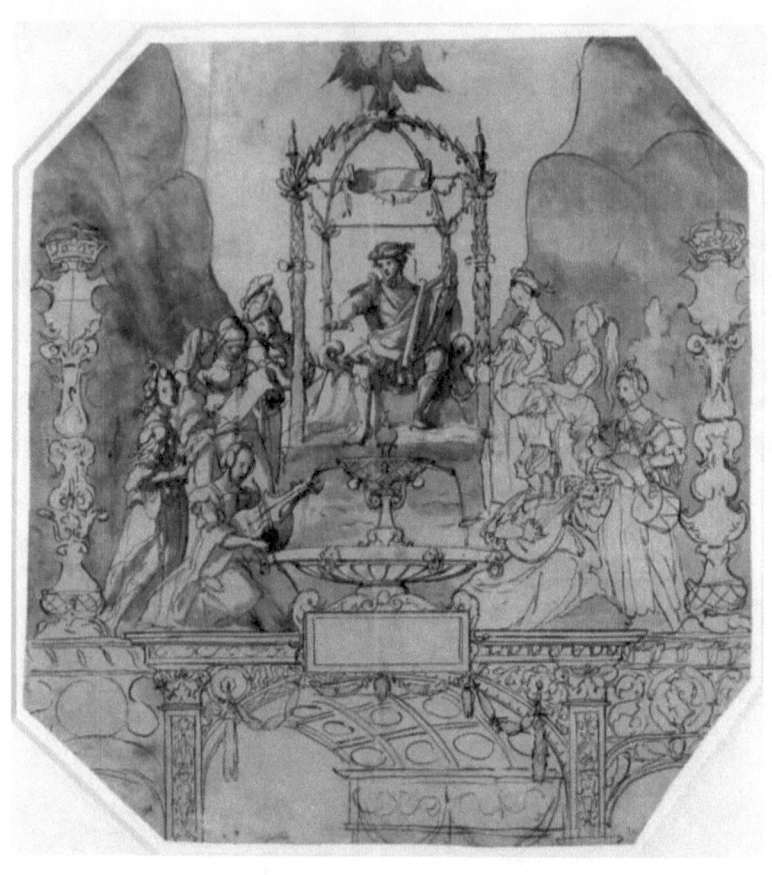

Apollo and the Muses on Parnassus, 1533
Pen in black, over traces of black pencil, with gray,
blue, and brown wash

The eve of Anne Boleyn's coronation on June 1, 1533, was celebrated with a festive procession in London. To pay their respects to the new queen, the members of the German Steelyard in London had a display erected, on the basis of a design by Holbein, representing Mount Parnassus, on which Apollo sat in stately splendour under a baldacchino in the company of the Muses. The reports of various eyewitnesses survive, who were particularly impressed that the Helicon spring was a fountain from which real Rhine wine flowed until evening.

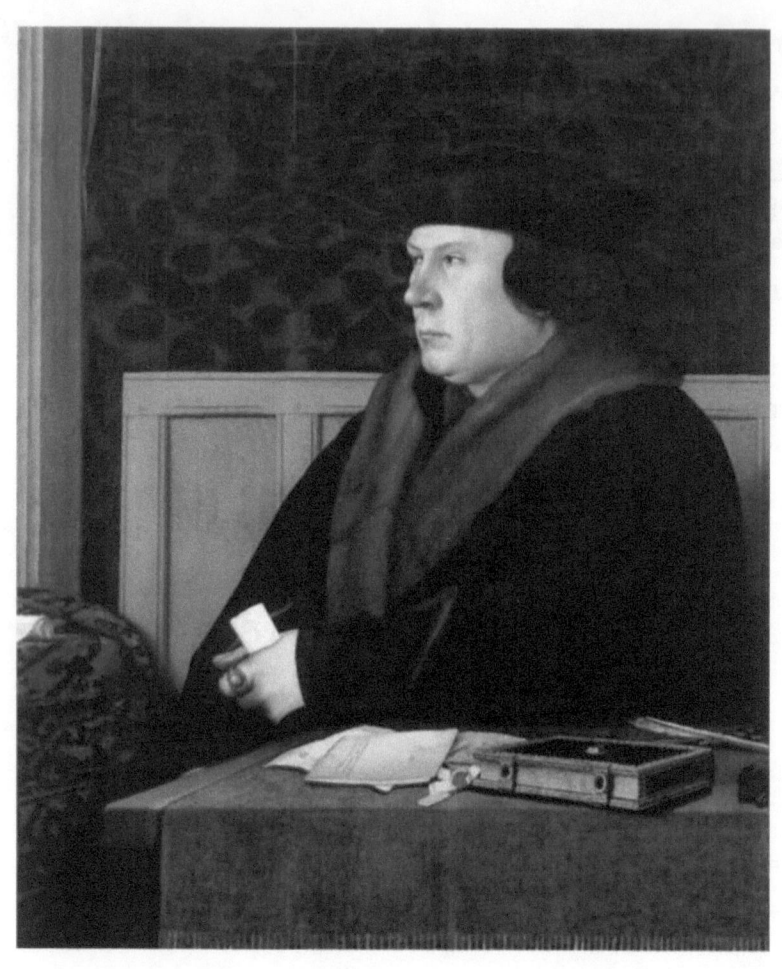

Portrait of Thomas Cromwell, c.1533
Oil on panel

Though Cromwell (c. 1485-1540) came from a modest background, he rose at court so successfully that he became the king's secretary and Chancellor of the Exchequer. It was he who suggested to Henry VIII that the king make himself head of the English Church. As Vicar General, Cromwell put into effect the Dissolution of the Monasteries. However, in 1540, he fell from favour with Henry and was executed. The inscription on the paper lying on the table describes Cromwell as "Master of the Jewell House," an official position that he occupied for one year from April 12, 1532.

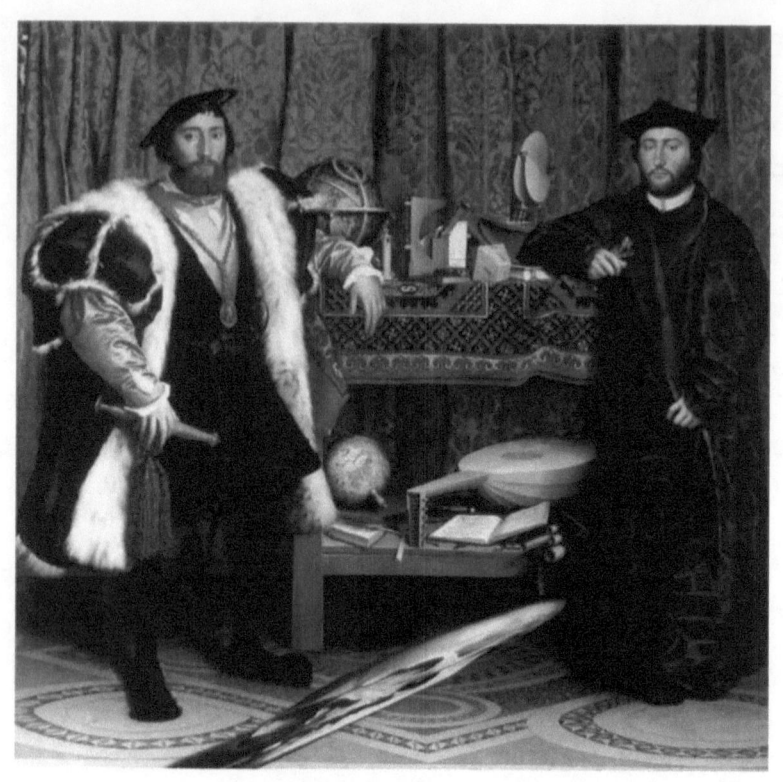

The Ambassadors, 1533
Oil on panel

This huge panel is one of the earliest portraits combining two full-length figures on the scale of life. A paean to two scholar-diplomats and to the artist's virtuosity, it is on closer examination a reminder also of the brevity of life and of the vanity of human accomplishments. While life is short, Holbein seems to say, art is long-lasting - but eternity endures for ever.

On our left stands Jean de Dinteville, a French nobleman posted to London as ambassador. The globe on the bottom shelf shows Polisy, where he had his château; the ornate sheath of the dagger in his right hand gives his age as 29. To his left stands his friend and fellow-countryman, Georges de Selve, whose visit to London in 1533 is commemorated here. A brilliant classical scholar, he had some years earlier been created Bishop of Lavaur. He leans his elbow on a book inscribed with his age: 25. In their attire, their poses and their bearing the two friends exemplify, respectively, the active and the contemplative life, which, together, complement each other.

On the what-not between them Holbein has depicted the wide range of their interests - a compendium of the culture of the age. On the top shelf, the minutely rendered `Turkey' carpet bears a celestial globe and an array of astronomical and navigational instruments. The cylindrical dial gives the date as 11 April; the polyhedral dial on the right indicates two different times of day. In front of the terrestrial globe on the lower shelf lies a German text-book of Arithmetic for Merchants, propped open with a T-square. A lute and a case of recorders or flutes demonstrate both Holbein's mastery of foreshortening and the sitters' musical interests. But a string of the lute has snapped a traditional emblem of fragility. Just visible in the top left corner, at the edge of the magnificently patterned green hanging, is a crucifix. The hymnal in front of the lute is open at Martin Luther's hymn,'Come Holy Ghost our souls inspire'. Christian faith offers hope of eternal life when dust returns to dust.

Across the mosaic floor - derived from the medieval pavement in Westminster Abbey - there spreads a curious shape between the two friends. It is a skull, skilfully distorted so that its true form can only be perceived from the correct viewpoint at the edges of the panel. The painting may have been intended to hang over a staircase so that viewers might see it when ascending or descending. Possibly referring to a personal device of Jean de Dinteville, whose cap medallion bears a skull, it is also the quintessential memento mori, reminder of mortality. In Holbein's meticulously real-seeming picture, the distortion also functions as a signal that reality, as perceived by the senses, must be viewed `correctly' to reveal its full meaning. A frontal nod of recognition at the worldly semblance of things is not enough.

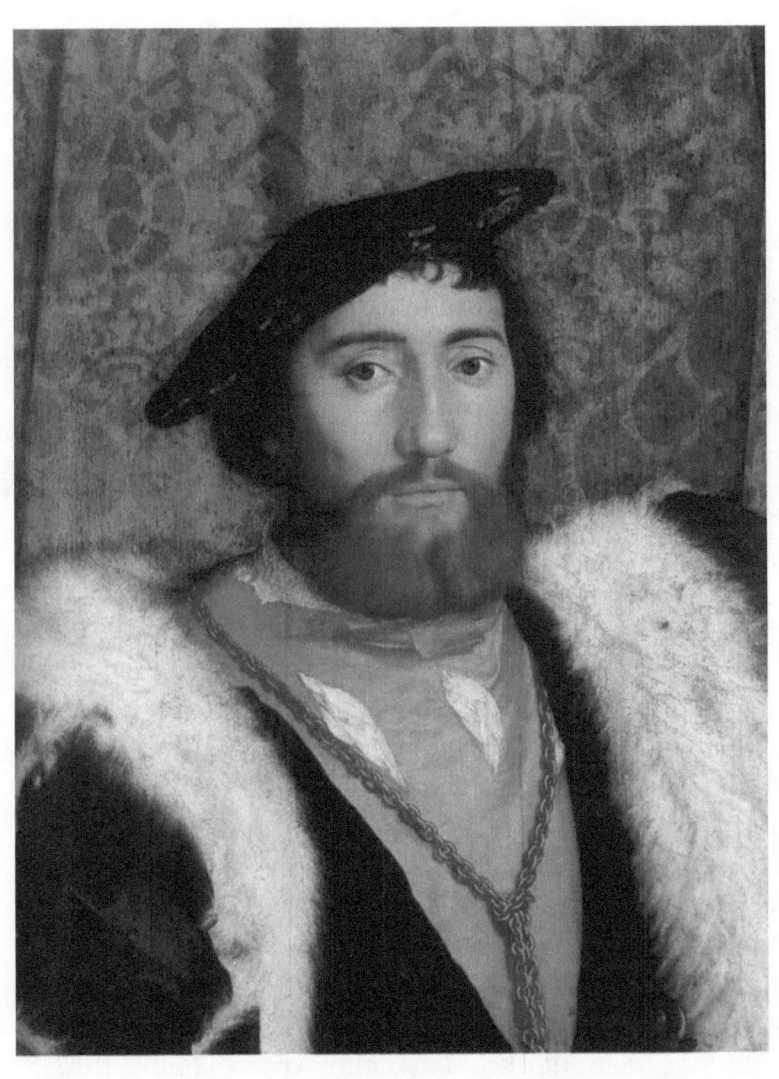

The Ambassadors (detail)

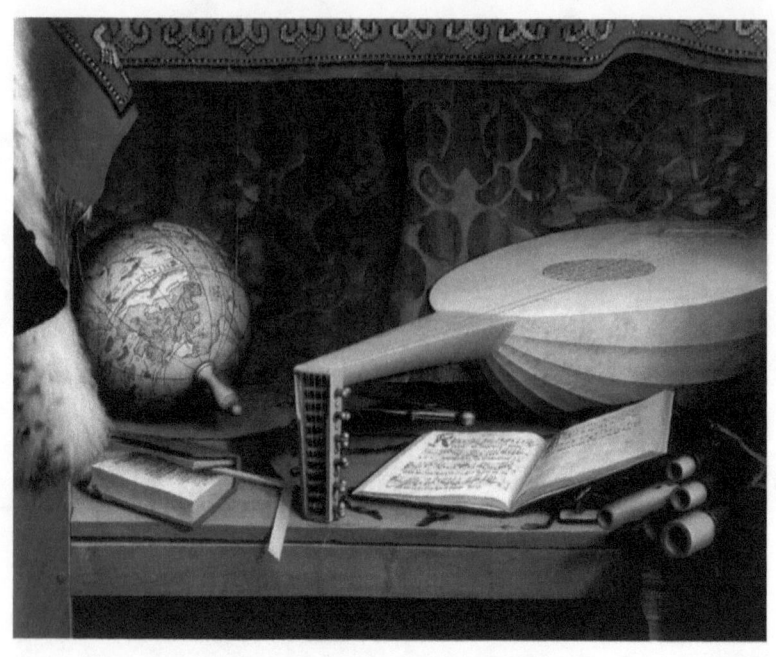

The Ambassadors (detail)

Whereas the astronomical globe on the upper shelf helps to identify the stars, the lower globe shows the Earth. In the centre, the word Polisy can be made out, the place where Jean de Dinteville had his château, for which the picture was intended. Besides this are two opened books, plus dividers, a lute with a broken string, and a bag with wooden flutes. The arithmetical book has been identified as Peter Apian's (1495-1552) book Eyn Newe unnd wohlgegrьndte underweysung aller Kauffmanss Rechnung (A new and thorough instruction in all mercantile calculations), published 1527, while the hymnal contains two songs from Johannes Walther's (1496-1570) Lutheran hymnal published in Wittenberg in 1524.

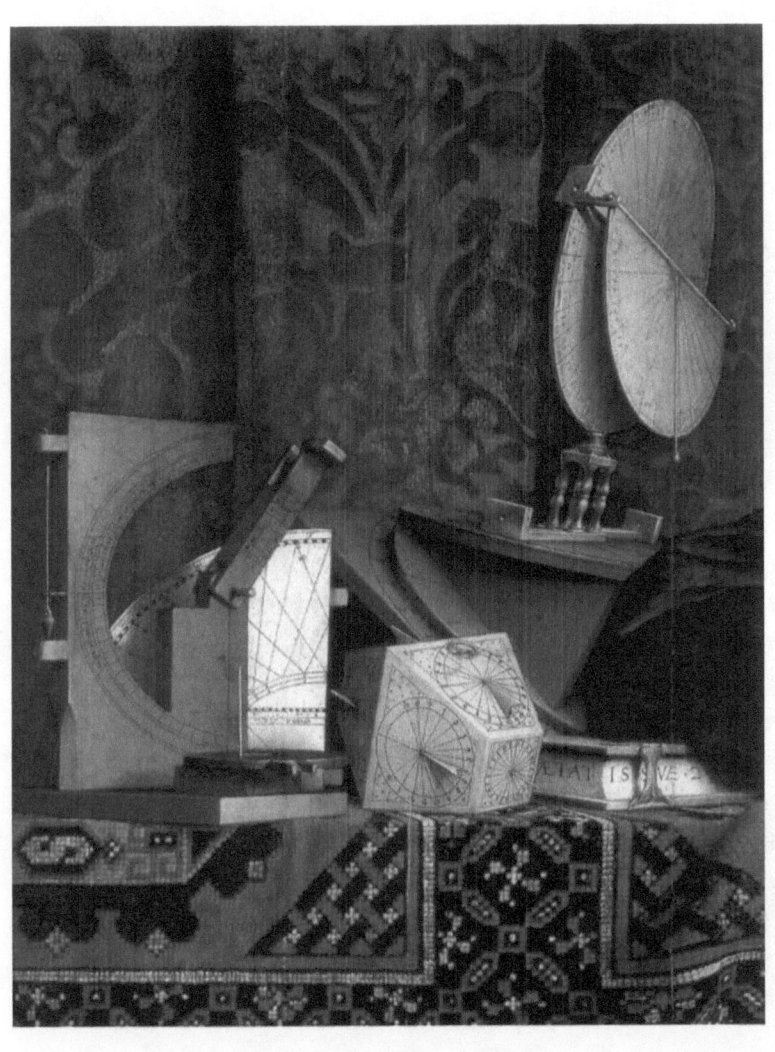

The Ambassadors (detail)

Hans Holbein's double portrait is an early example of the friendship portrait. It depicts the two French ambassadors to the English court, Jean de Dinteville (1504-1555) and Georges de Selve (1508/09-1541). Dinteville, who spent many years in London, probably commissioned the painting to record his friend's visit at Easter 1533. His own figure displays great worldly pomp, wearing an opulent, fur-lined coat and decorated with the Order of St. Michael, while de Selve's clothes, at least in colour, are more restrained. His full-length robe is the appropriate dress for a Bishop of Lavour, an office he had entered upon in 1526, when he was not much older than eighteen.

The two, almost life-sized figures of the ambassadors are shown leaning against a two-storey cupboard, the upper of whose two shelves is spread with a rug, before a green damask curtain. The floor design imitates a mosaic in the sanctuary at Westminster Cathedral, laid by Italian craftsmen at the beginning of the fourteenth century. This shows that Holbein's painting, though appearing to imitate reality with almost photographic attention to detail, is not merely a "reproduction" of reality, but an "invented" composition, calculated to portray persons and objects as ideal types.

As is often the case in Holbein's portraits (compare his portrait of Georg Gisze), the objects on the shelves refer to the intellectual interests and professional and practical activities of the sitters. The instruments and books displayed reflect the design of the cupboard itself in that those on the upper shelf would be used for the study of the heavens and heavenly bodies (celestial globe, compasses, sundial, cylindrical calendar, level and quadrant), while the objects on the lower shelf have more to do with everyday worldly matters. Thus, on the left - next to the worldly-minded Dinteville - is an open copy of Peter Apian's book of calculations for merchants (published in Ingolstadt, 1527), and on the right - near the bishop - a copy of Johann Walther's "Geystliches Gesangbьchlein" (Hymnal) (Wittenberg 1524), containing Luther's hymns. The globe itself, an exact copy of Johann Schцner's globe of 1523, documents their interest in geography, which, due to discoveries made at the turn of the century, had become an increasingly central aspect of humanist scholarship. The cumulative effect of the objects is to demonstrate the ambassadors' close association to the scientific and educational community of the Renaissance, a movement considered highly "progressive" at the time. Although religious motifs are present here, they are given secondary status. This testifies to the placatory, tolerant attitude of the Catholic bishop, who, during a period of bitter religious strife, sought to reconcile the confessions. His attitude is documented by two of Luther's hymns in Walther's hymnal. His desire for harmony is echoed in the symbolic presence of the lute. Enlightened humanism had come to see religion as an ethical guide in matters of conduct: it was essential to develop an empirical awareness of physical reality; equally, it was important to be aware of the brevity of life and, constantly, to reckon with death's intervention.

This explains the reason for the anamorphic skull Holbein has painted rising diagonally from the bottom left of the canvas. Its real presence in the ambassadors' world is underlined by the heavy shadow it casts on the floor. Earlier portraitists, Barthel Bruyn for example, had showed the skull, a symbol of the vanity of all worldly things, on the reverse of their paintings, anticipating of the future state of the sitter portrayed on the obverse. Here, however, the skull is less an occult symbol, than lived presence: the cause, no doubt, of the melancholic moods of which Dinteville is reputed to have so often complained. His friend's visit was particularly important to him during such a period of depression. At a time when the state had begun to determine the legal contours of social institutions such as marriage, the relative independence of friendship and the opportunity it afforded for the unsanctioned exchange of feelings and views became more and more important. The terms in which Michel de Montaigne later praised friendship in his "Essais" are therefore hardly surprising: "Each friend entrusts himself so completely to the other, that he has nought left to give to a third."

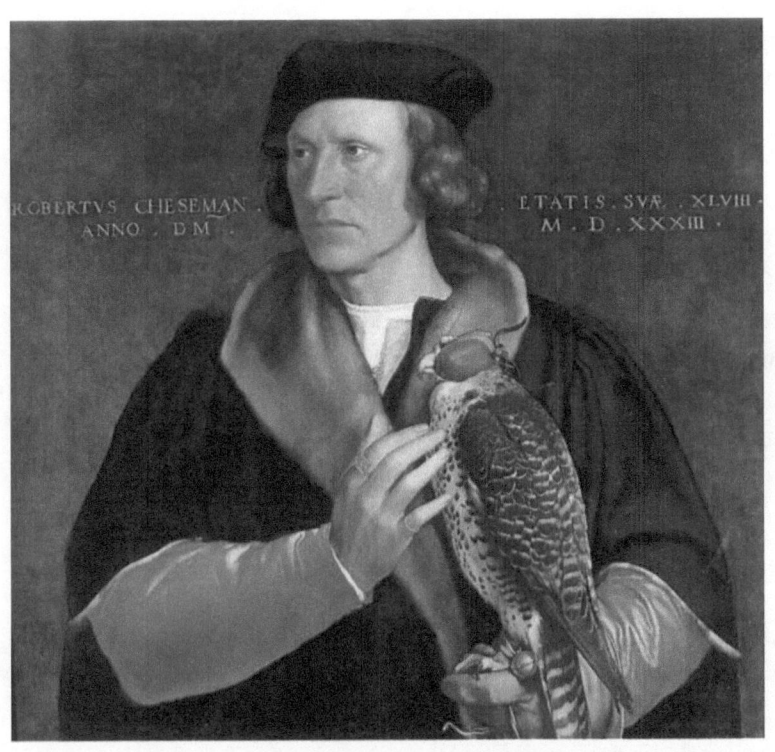

Robert Cheseman, 1533
Oil on oak

Robert Cheseman (1485-1547) was an influential figure
in Middlesex, where he was responsible for
marshalling levies. He more than once raised troops for
Henry VIII's campaigns. Along with other minor
figures at court, many of whom were to rise with the
fortunes of Thomas Cromwell in the 1530s, Cheseman
was the sort of patron on whom Holbein concentrated
during the first few years of his second English sojourn.
Such clients were less in evidence once Henry and his
royal entourage had adopted `the Apelles of our time'.

These English sitters had more limited intellectual aims in mind for their portraits than the foreign merchants or ambassadors in London. The need for clear, effective portrayal, shorn of symbolism (and expensively painted detail) perhaps accounts for the innovatory use of the information about the sitter that floats in gold lettering on the blue background a feature more familiar in miniatures. The artist's regressive abandonment of spatially interesting, illusionistic backgrounds may be another indicator of the undeveloped taste of English clients - a full native understanding of perspective construction did not arise until Inigo Jones' theatre-design work around 1615. Cheseman had himself painted holding a falcon. The head of the bird is capped, because the falcon is not supposed to see anything until the falconer sets him at a target. Cheseman appears to be looking for just such a target, his gaze apparently scanning the distance, beyond the pictorial field.

The very fine portrayal of the falcon shows Holbein's great power in observing nature; the bird's presence, signifying Cheseman's wish to show his social status, neatly serves to illustrate human nature.

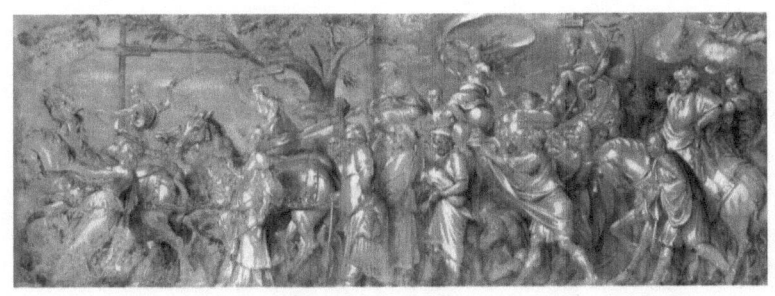

The Triumph of Riches, 1532-34
Pen and brown ink with washes, chalk and bodycolour

This, and its pendant the Triumph of Poverty, originally hung in the Great Hall of the German Steelyard in Blackfriars, London, even after Elizabeth I rescinded the company's privileges during the post-Armada surge of nationalism in 1589. In about December 1609 the works were presented to Henry, Prince of Wales (who died in 1612) and thence entered the Earl of Arundel's collection in Holland via Charles I in 1641. They were destroyed by fire at Kremsier Castle in 1752. Two sets of copies now exist, of which the coloured version by Lucas Vorsterman the Elder in Oxford is considered the most accurate.

The Triumphs give evidence that Holbein's continental interest in allegorical presentation, which frequently overflowed into his portraiture, was maintained in England despite the paucity of native interest in the increasingly reformist climate. The works functioned as a moral admonition to the denizens of the Steelyard, much as the allegorical designs often displayed in law-courts defined the qualities required of legal administrators.

Ancient Plutus, god of riches, is drawn along by
wealthy men before who blindfolded Fortuna throws
money. The horses, as vices (for example, Avarice) are
controlled by the virtues needed when wealth comes
one's way. The Latin inscription, at one time ascribed to
More, translates as `Gold is the father of deceit and the
child of grief. He who lacks it is in sorrow; he who
possesses it is fearful'. Mantegna can be cited as a
visual source, primarily his Triumph of Caesar panels
(now at Hampton Court), which Holbein probably
knew through engravings.

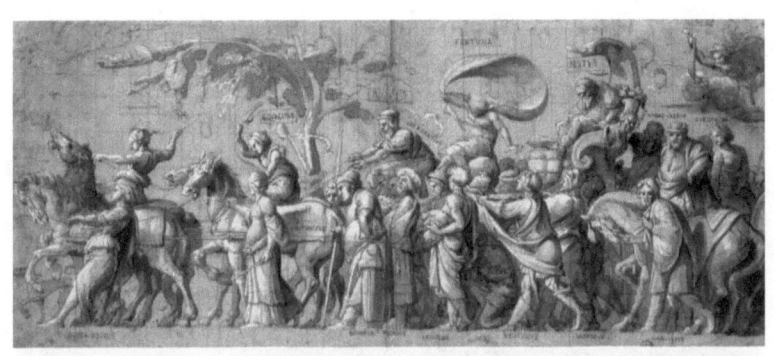

Triumph of Wealth, 1532-34
Pen in brown, with gray and brown wash, white
highlights and subsequently squared

Plutus, the old, frail god of wealth, sits on a triumphal
chariot drawn by four horses. Reason (Ratio) steers the
chariot with Knowledge (Notitia) and Will (Voluntas).
The horses - Avarice, Fraud, Usury, and Contract - are
held in check by four women, who stand for Generosity
(Liberalitas), Honesty (Bona Fides), Balance
(Aequalitas), and Justice (Iustitia). Goddess of fortune,
Fortuna, sits on the wagon with full sail and bound
eyes, and apportions her wealth blindly to a group of
people accompanying the chariot. Their good or bad
luck was determined by the caprice of lottery. Nemesis,
the goddess of Revenge, flies in the clouds behind as
the embodiment of the inexorableness of fate. She
makes it clear that even men and women particularly
favoured in life, like Croesus, Midas, and Cleopatra,
who are following the procession on horseback,
ultimately come to a fall.

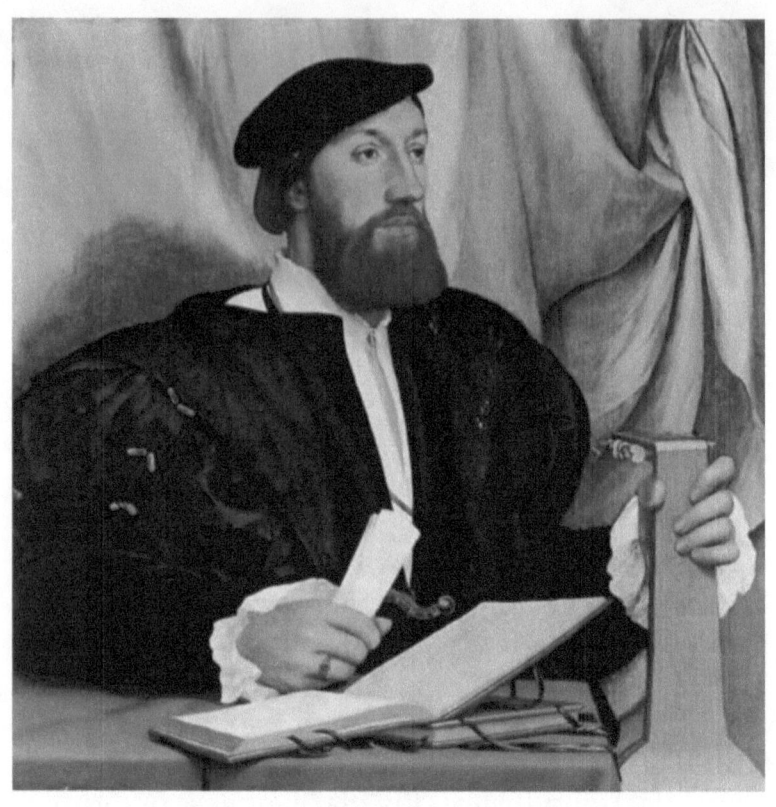

Unknown gentleman with music books and lute, c.1534
Oil on panel

The painting's similarities with other works dating
from the early 1530s have led to the supposition that
the sitter was a leading musician at Henry VIII's court.
The king was a keen musician and amateur composer
and rewarded such figures well; to be afforded the
distinction of a Holbein portrait could be seen as an
official seal of approval. The sitter's employment
demonstrates the range of clientele to whom Holbein
now catered.

Time has not been kind to this work, however, much of whose detail has been destroyed by overzealous cleaning. The green background is that of the underpainting - hence its unusually harsh tone - and definition on the lute is vague. It is to be expected that writing was originally visible on the score, which may have given the identity of the sitter (once thought to be Jean de Dinteville).

The structure and pose show Holbein's knowledge of current Venetian compositional formations (as exemplified in the work of Titian and Lotto).

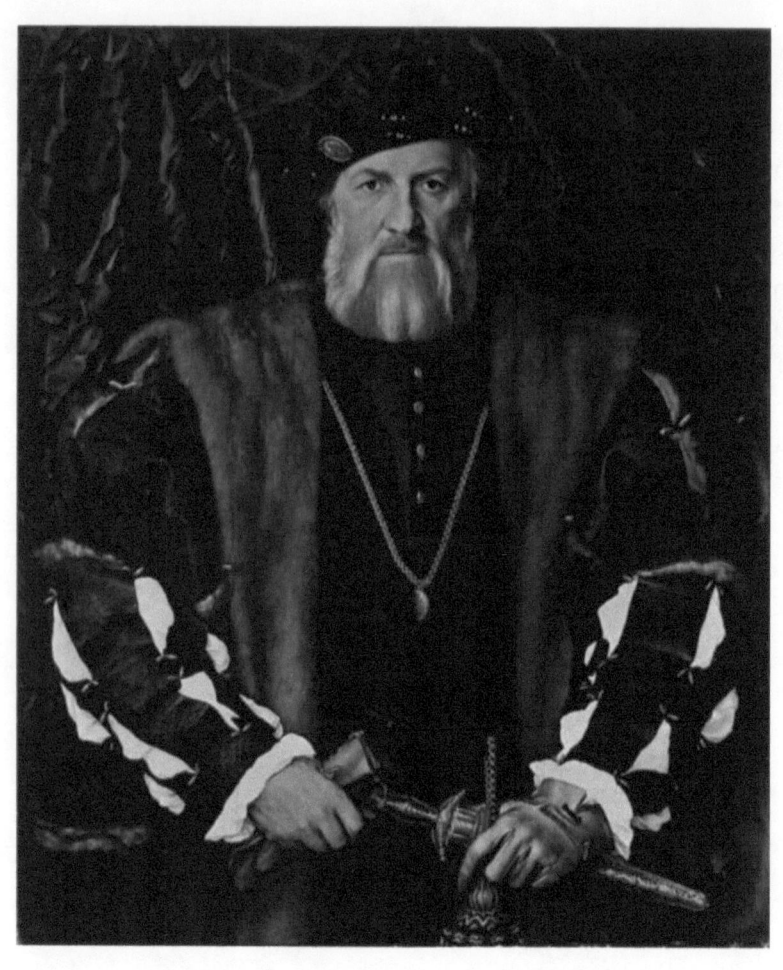

Portrait of Charles de Solier, c.1535
Oil on canvas

Born about 1480, the French ambassador Charles de Solier remained in London from April 3 to July 26, 1534, during which time Holbein must have painted this portrait. As the name of the man is not written on the painting, it was forgotten over the centuries, and until the 19th century even the painter was not known. Consequently, when Augustus III of Saxony (elector 1733-1763) acquired the panel in 1746, it was described as a portrait of the ruler of Milan, Ludovico Sforza, Il Moro (duke 1481-1499), painted by Leonardo da Vinci.

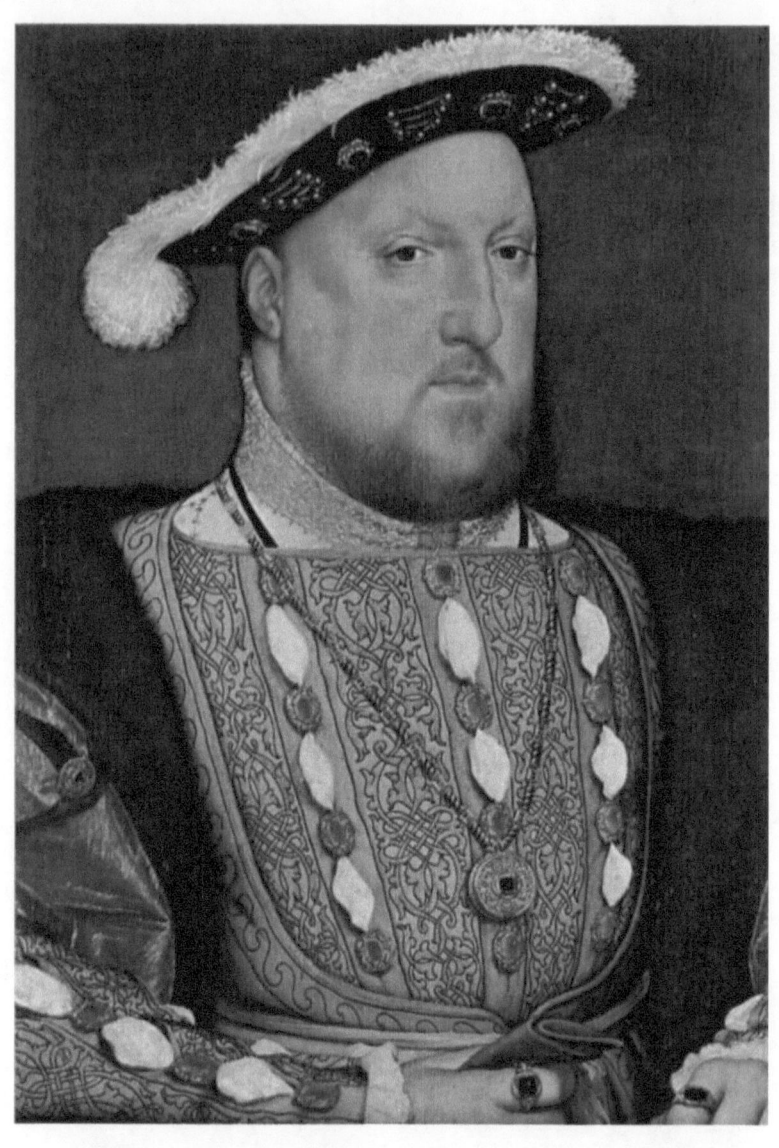

Portrait of Henry VIII, King of England, c.1535
Oil on panel

Henry VIII (1491-1547), king of England (1509-47), who presided over the beginnings of the English Renaissance and the English Reformation. His six wives were, successively, Catherine of Aragon (the mother of the future queen Mary I), Anne Boleyn (the mother of the future queen Elizabeth I), Jane Seymour (the mother of Henry's successor, Edward VI), Anne of Cleves, Catherine Howard, and Catherine Parr.

This portrait is the only surviving individual portrait of Henry that Holbein himself painted. In terms of features, it corresponds largely to the figure in the Whitehall cartoon. Both portraits are likely to have been based on a single, now lost portrait study by Holbein. However, as a consequence of the small format of the panel painting, the heavy shoulder chain that the king wears in the monumental portrait is omitted here, and his sleeves are embroidered with a very delicate gold thread.

This is the quintessential image of the overbearing and tyrannous monarch, from the year the dissolution of the monasteries (and the consequent appropriation of their wealth for the Crown and its servants) was instigated. Holbein depicts the King at `face value', without flattery, emphasizing the small, humourless eyes and mouth, the curiously flat cheeks and chin. Henry's bulky and capricious authority haunts the work despite its small size. Its condensation of magnificence run riot here takes the form of real gold used in the chain, jewellery and collar.

The portrait is undoubtedly a tour de force; after its execution, Holbein's position at the court seems to have been secure, and he was used as a painter-ambassador when the King's marital plans unraveled in the late 1530s. Only his misleading portrayal of Anne of Cleves would check his popularity.

The subsequent spawning of similar but less effective portraits of the king by Holbein's followers has tended to obscure the compelling mixture of simplicity and realism displayed in this design - the tilt and curve of the black and white hat, the fearful symmetry of the jewelled jacket and the modelling of the hands: imitators often managed either simplicity or realism but never both.

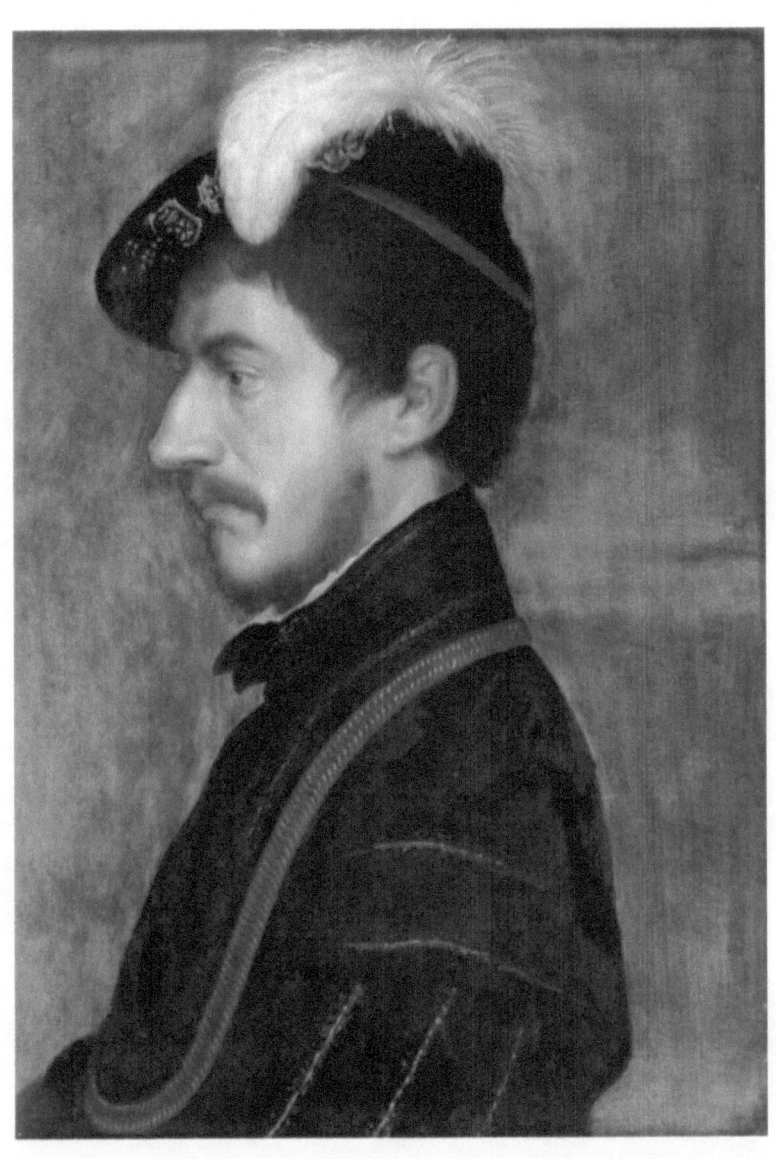

Portrait of Sir Nicholas Poyntz, 1535
Oil on panel

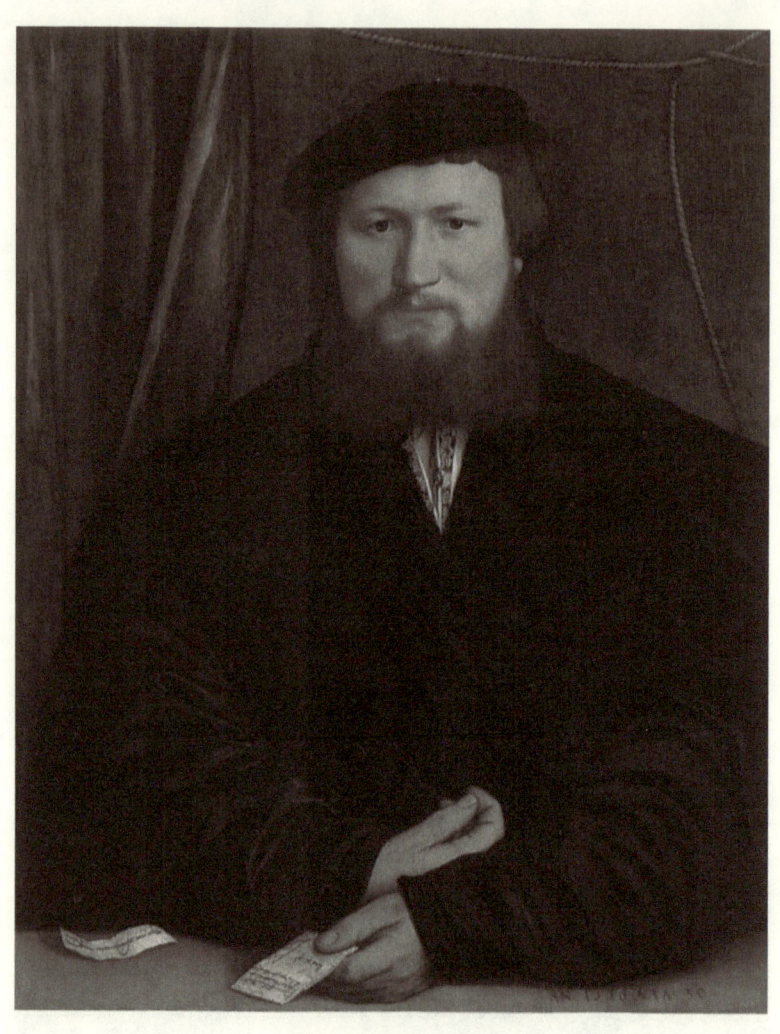

Derek Berck, 1536
Oil on canvas

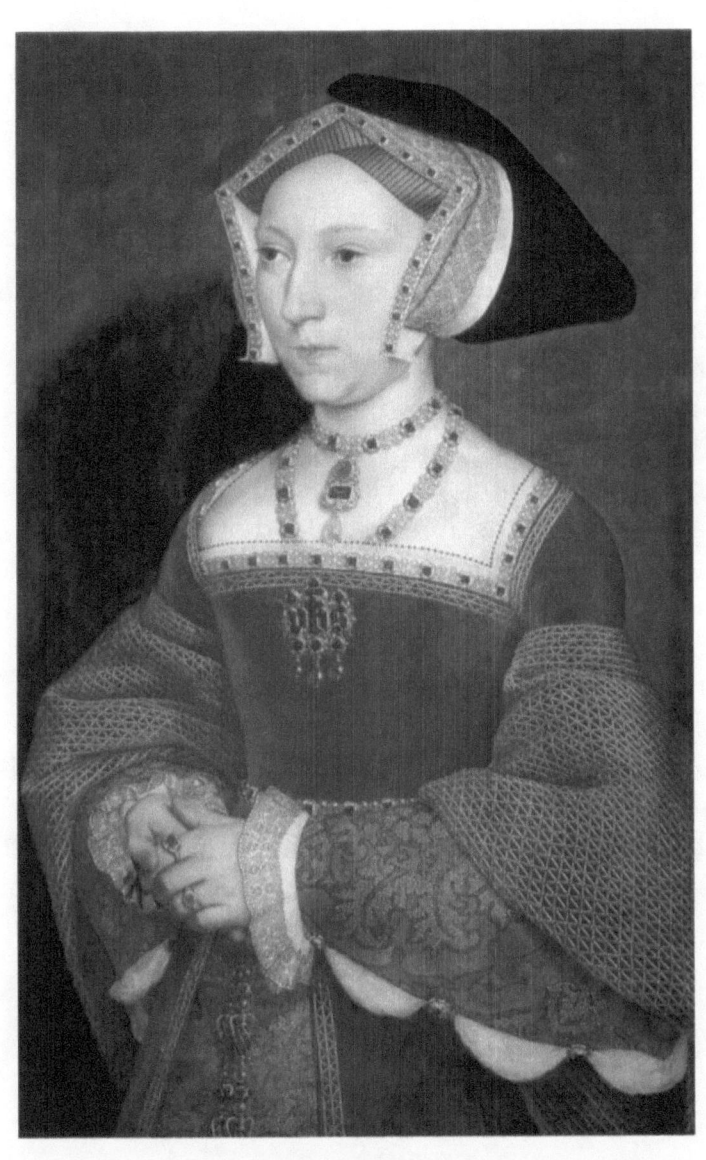

Jane Seymour, 1536
Oil on panel

Jane Seymour (1509-1537) was the third wife of King Henry VIII of England and mother of King Edward VI. She succeeded - where Henry's previous wives had failed - in providing a legitimate male heir to the throne.

Jane's father was Sir John Seymour of Wolf Hall, Savernake, Wiltshire. She became a lady in waiting to Henry's first wife, Catherine of Aragon, and then to Anne Boleyn, who married the King in 1533. Henry probably became attracted to Jane in 1535, when he visited her father at Wolf Hall, but, though willing to marry him, she refused to be his mistress. That determination undoubtedly helped bring about Anne Boleyn's downfall and execution (May 19, 1536). On May 30, 1536, Henry and Jane were married privately. During the remaining 17 months of her life Jane managed to restore Mary, Henry's daughter by Catherine of Aragon, to the King's favour. Mary was a Roman Catholic, and some scholars have interpreted Jane's intercession to mean that she had little sympathy with the English Reformation. The future Edward VI was born on October 12, 1537, but, to Henry's genuine sorrow, Jane died 12 days later.

Holbein executed this portrait shortly after the marriage of Henry VIII and Jane Seymour. In attitude and expression, the Seymour portrait matches that in the Whitehall composition, but the portraits differ in the arrangement of the bonnet veil; this individual portrait follows the preparatory study in the Royal Collection in Windsor Castle. This change is important only from a compositional point of view, and probably derived from Holbein himself. However, the major changes in tonality and patterns in Jane's gown will probably have been undertaken only after consultation with the client.

Holbein's portrait depicts a figure frozen in an official sense of responsibility. The simplicity of the shadowed background accentuates the increasing richness and boldness of design and adornment in Henrician court fashion, and the artist's skill is pre-eminent in creating the sheen and lustre of the precious stones. Great attention has been paid to the realism of the silver thread in the queen's dress, and this new opulence was to be echoed in the portrait of Henry himself.

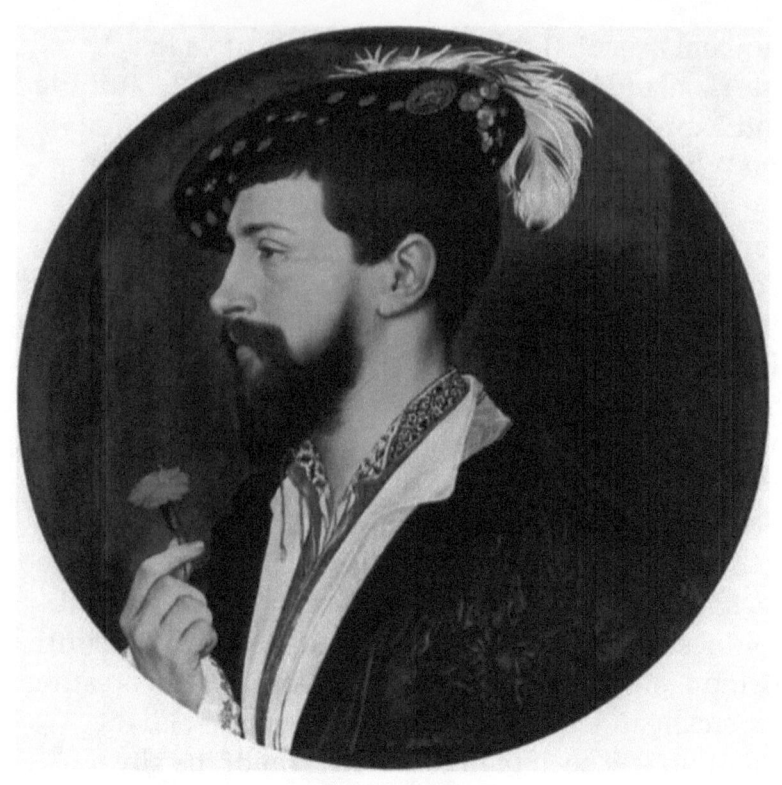

Portrait of Simon George of Quocote, c.1536
Oil on panel

At the other end of the spectrum of portraiture from the blatant display of regal power in Henry VIII's portrait (Museo Thyssen-Bornemisza, Madrid), is the aesthetic delicacy and reverie of this circular portrait. It is also Holbein's only profile portrait. A minor court figure, Simon George sports a fashionable hat similar to the King's, a hat whose circularity echoes that of the work itself.

Holbein had avoided the profile hitherto in England since it reduced the scope for his sharp yet reticent portrayal of personality. After Holbein's death, this format became popular for a while among his followers, perhaps for the very reason that it made a less searching examination of their ability to express psychological nuance.

The humour in the eyes and some inscrutable edge of a smile about the mouth is remarkably conveyed here, although these qualities had been lacking in the blunt preliminary drawing.

The carnation held by the sitter in his right hand is a reference to an engagement or marriage. The identification with Simon George is based on an inscription on the relevant portrait study in the Royal Collection in Windsor Castle, which notes that Simon comes from Cornwall. Otherwise little is known about him.

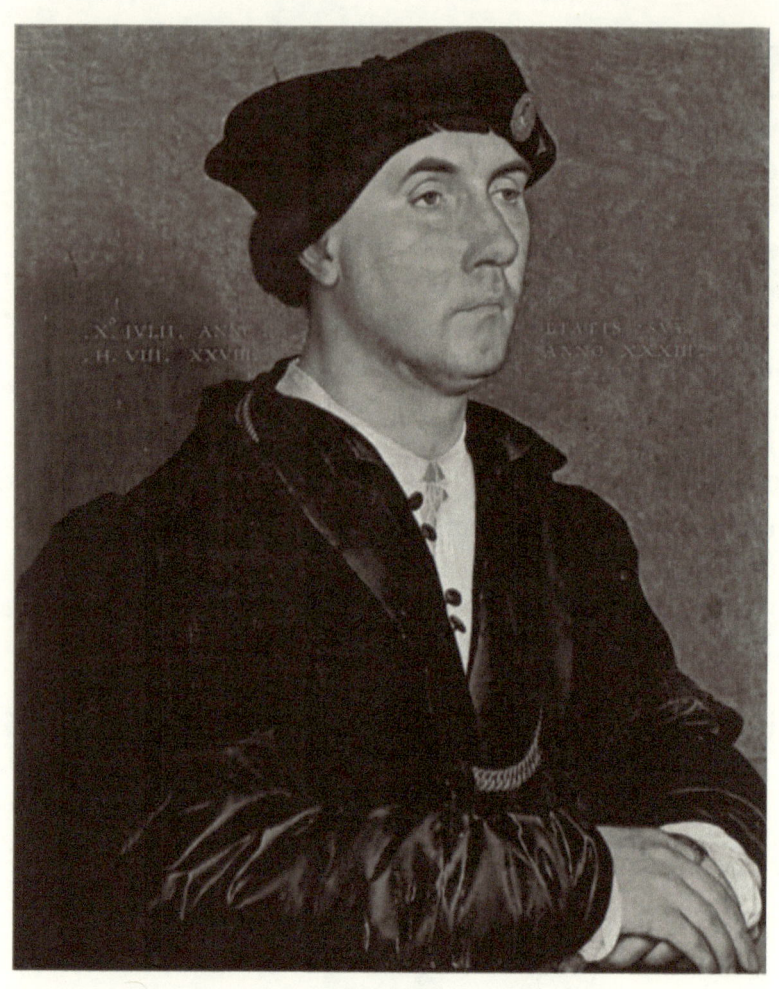

Portrait of Sir Richard Southwell, 1536
Oil on panel

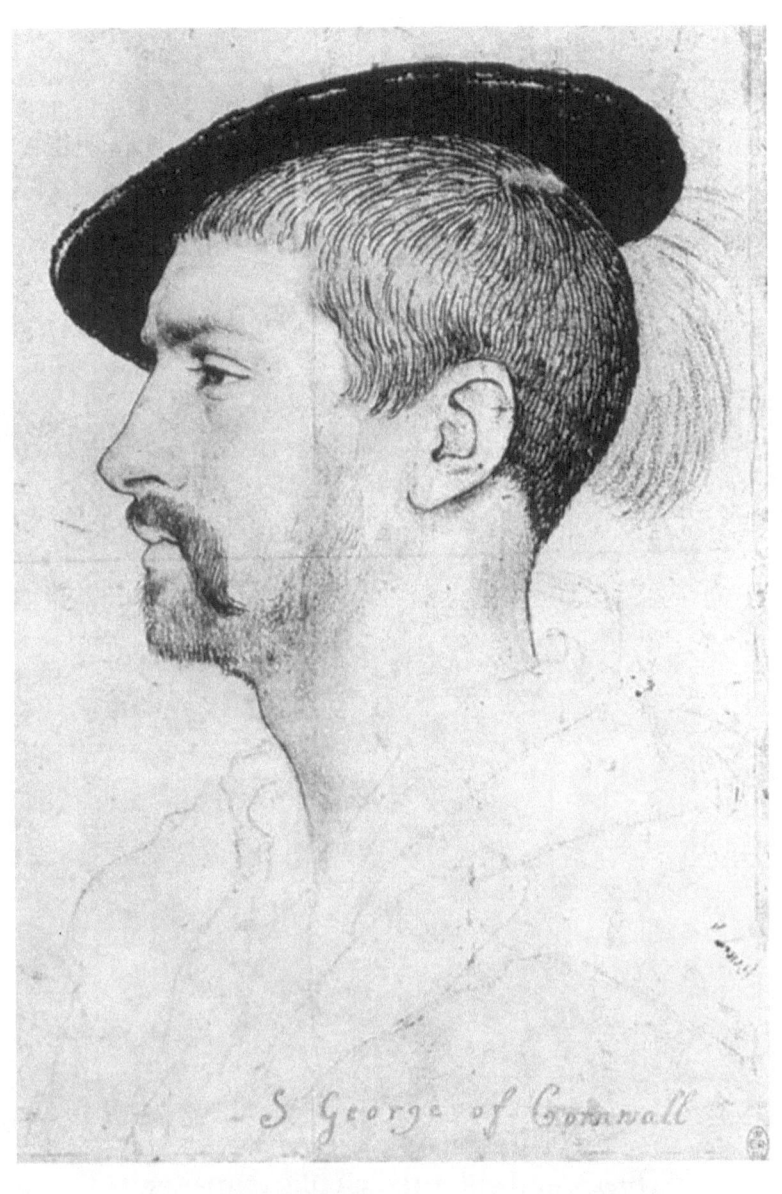

Simon George of Quocote, 1536
Pale pink priming, chalk with indian ink

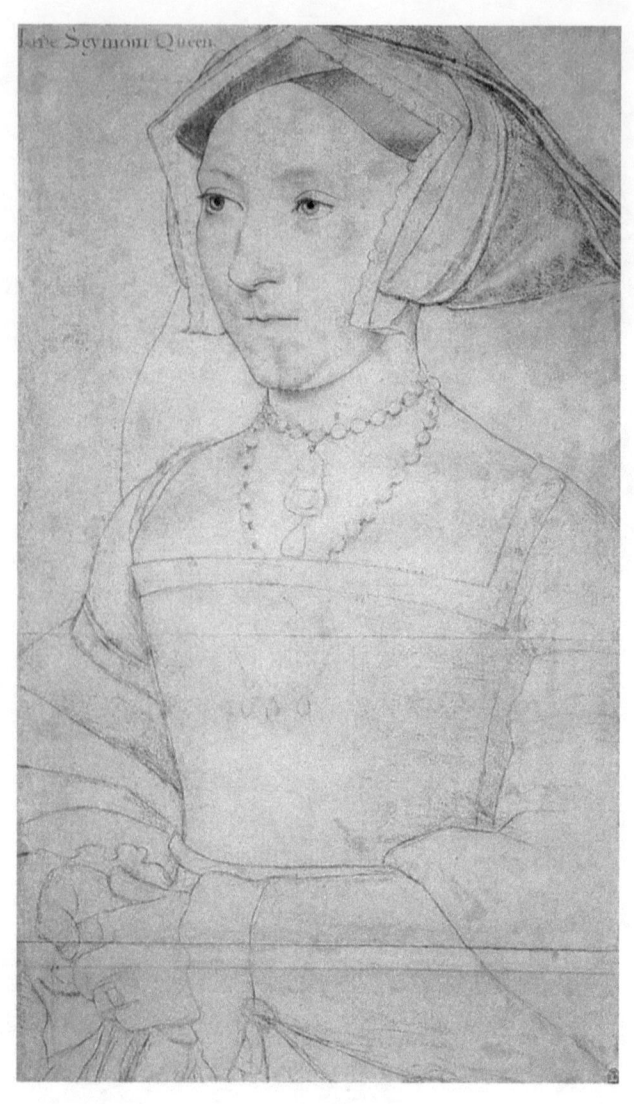

Jane Seymour, 1536-37
Black and coloured chalks on paper,

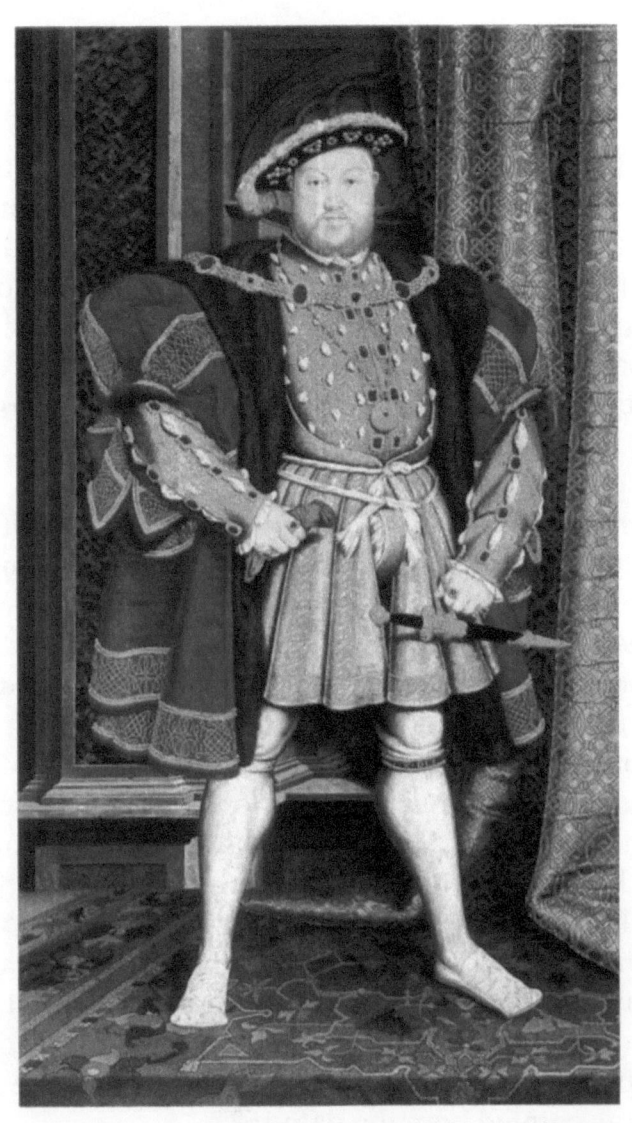

Henry VIII, c.1537
Oil on canvas

The top job of Holbein, the court painter, was quite certainly to paint the king's portrait. In the 1530s, Henry VIII had enlarged his London residence Whitehall Palace, and needed a grand picture for it. It was to feature not only him and his wife Jane Seymour, but also his parents, the first Tudor monarchs, and was also intended to proclaim the fame of the ruling house in word and image. Since the composition probably adorned one wall of the Privy Chamber, a private chamber accessible only to more intimate members of court, the picture was not aimed at a broad public but a select group at court.

No contract for the mural survives, but Henry VIII must have commissioned it in the short time during which he was married to Jane Seymour, in other words between May 30, 1536, and October 12, 1537. Both Catharine of Aragon and Anne Boleyn were already dead; in showing Jane together with Elizabeth of York and the Tudor monarchs in the picture, Henry's new connection was presented as the only legitimate one and the children of the marriage as the only rightful heirs. Possibly the picture was commissioned shortly after the wedding: in the surviving section of the cartoon a cartouche is included in the frieze, displaying the initials of Henry and Jane linked in a love knot. According to the copy by the painter Remigius van Leemput (1607-1675) in 1667, the cartouche on the mural as painted bore the date 1537.

The picture shows a copy of the figure of Henry VIII from the left side of the mural which was destroyed in the Whitehall fire in 1698.

Henry VIII stands in the foreground like a colossus with legs apart and knees straight. His broad shoulders, emphasized by his heavy clothing, exaggerate the already unusual physical presence of this large man, whose sex is additionally stressed by a prominent girdle and codpiece. The king thus appears as the epitome of vigour and potency. This stance, with legs apart and knees locked straight, is very uncommon for the portrait of a king. The reason may be that at the time spread legs were considered improper, as the Frankfurt scholar Jodocus Willich (1501-1552) explains in a treatise on gestures first published in Basel in 1540. However, in visual art the stance was also associated with triumphant heroes; St. George, for example, can stand in a comparable pose after overcoming the dragon.

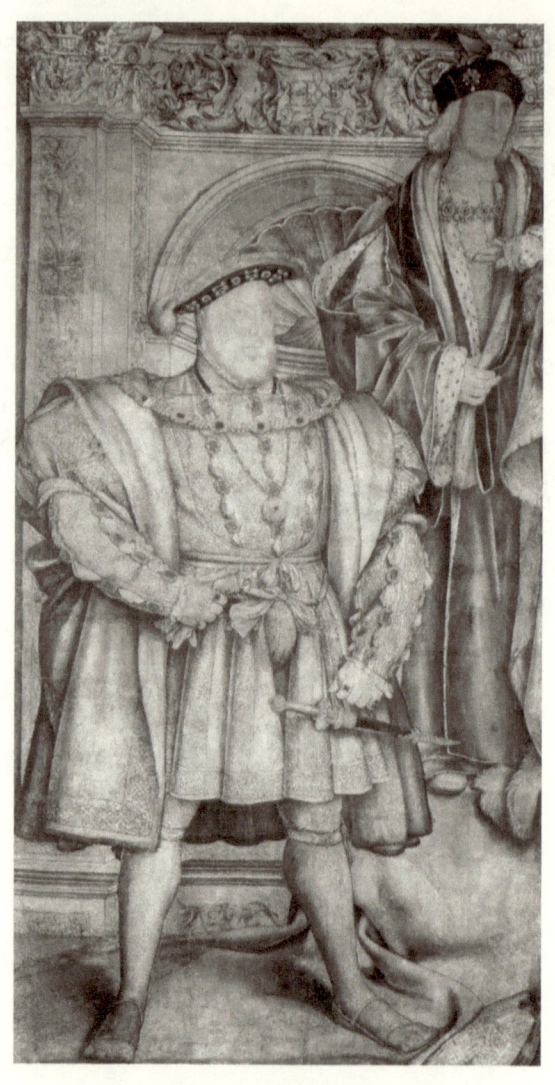

Henry VIII and Henry VII, 1537
Pen in black, with gray, brown, black, and red wash,
paper mounted on canvas

his cartoon is a section of a drawing for the wall painting in Whitehall, originally three times as large but to the same scale. However, unlike in the wall painting as finally executed, where Henry has his head turned frontally to the viewer, the cartoon shows Holbein planning a three quarters profile. The cartoon was used to transfer the picture to the wall, a needle being used to make holes along the outlines through which a fine charcoal powder was blown or dabbed after the cartoon has been fixed to the wall.

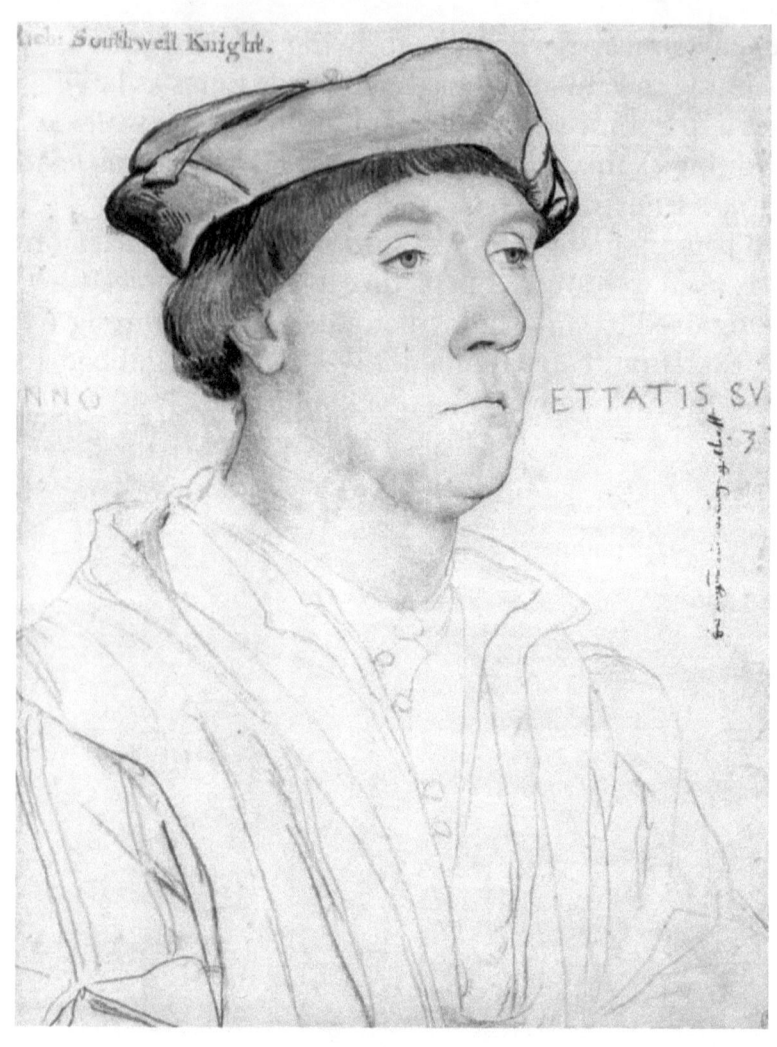

Portrait of Sir Richard Southwell, c. 1537
Black and coloured chalks, brush in black and metal
pen

Holbein did the study, which is a preparatory drawing for the portrait, in black, brown and yellow chalks and added emphasis with black ink. The paper was tinted pink, which is a technique he used only during his second visit to England. Before that, he never used colour grounds on paper nor mixed chalk and ink. In the righthand margin, Holbein notes in German that the eyes are slightly yellowish.

A comparison between the drawing and the finished portrait of Southwell (Uffizi, Florence) shows how complete Holbein's conceptions were before the painting was undertaken. Although corrections were sometimes made on the panel, the notation of light and shadow (down the back of Southwell's neck, for example) and such identifying features as the scar on his throat, were pinpointed from the start with such authority that the static massed volume of the sitter was fully in realized before paint was applied.

The face is changed very little between the two works - it is the garment that is altered; and from its monochrome sobriety the painting gains a simplified power that is the hallmark of the mid-1530s work.

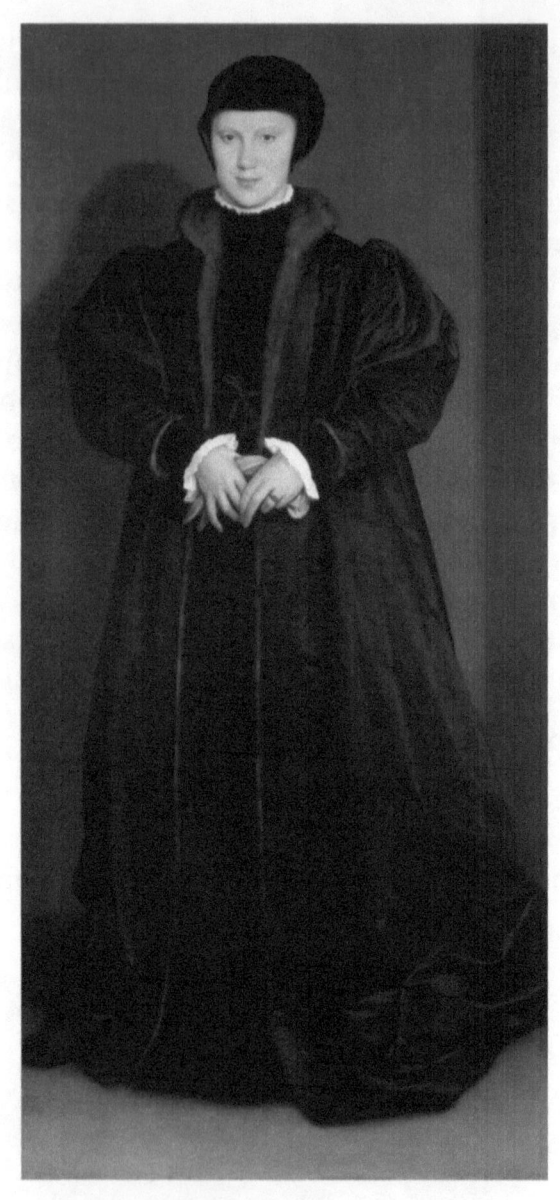

Christina of Denmark, c.1538
Oil on panel

Holbein's painting of the sixteen-year-old Christina of Denmark, widowed Duchess of Milan, is his only surviving full-length portrait of a woman. Remarkably for a work of this period, we know precisely how and when it came to be made. The younger daughter of King Christian II of Denmark, an early Lutheran sympathiser who lost his throne in 1523, she had been brought up in the Netherlands at the courts of her great-aunt, Margaret of Austria, Governess of the Netherlands until her death in 1530, and her aunt, Mary of Hungary, Margaret's successor and sister of the Emperor Charles V. After her husband's death in 1535, Christina returned to Brussels. Henry VIII of England attempted, unsuccessfully in the event, to marry her as his fourth wife after the death of Jane Seymour. On 12 March 1538 she agreed to sit for Holbein for three hours, and the English envoy judged the resulting drawing or drawings to be `very perfect'. Holbein must have worked up the painted portrait after his return to London, and the king was said to be `in love' with Christina, whom of course he had never met except through Holbein's art. It has been suggested that the full-face pose, characteristic of Holbein's other portraits of Henry's prospective brides, was chosen on instructions from the king, who may have felt that any other view might allow blemishes to be concealed from him.

The figure stands out isolated against the plain but brightly coloured background relieved only by shadows, cast not merely by Christina herself but by an unseen window frame. Since the black mourning dress carried no ornament, Holbein stressed the three-dimensional modelling, creating enlivening patterns from the reflection of light on the folds of the silken robe. Not known as a great beauty, Christina was, however, much praised for the elegance of her hands, and in this area of the painting Holbein suggests the different textures of linen, velvet, fur, leather, gold and gemstone to set off the delicate beauty of the flesh. Christina's faint smile seems at once demure and intimate. Generations of viewers have shared Henry's infatuation with this engaging portrait.

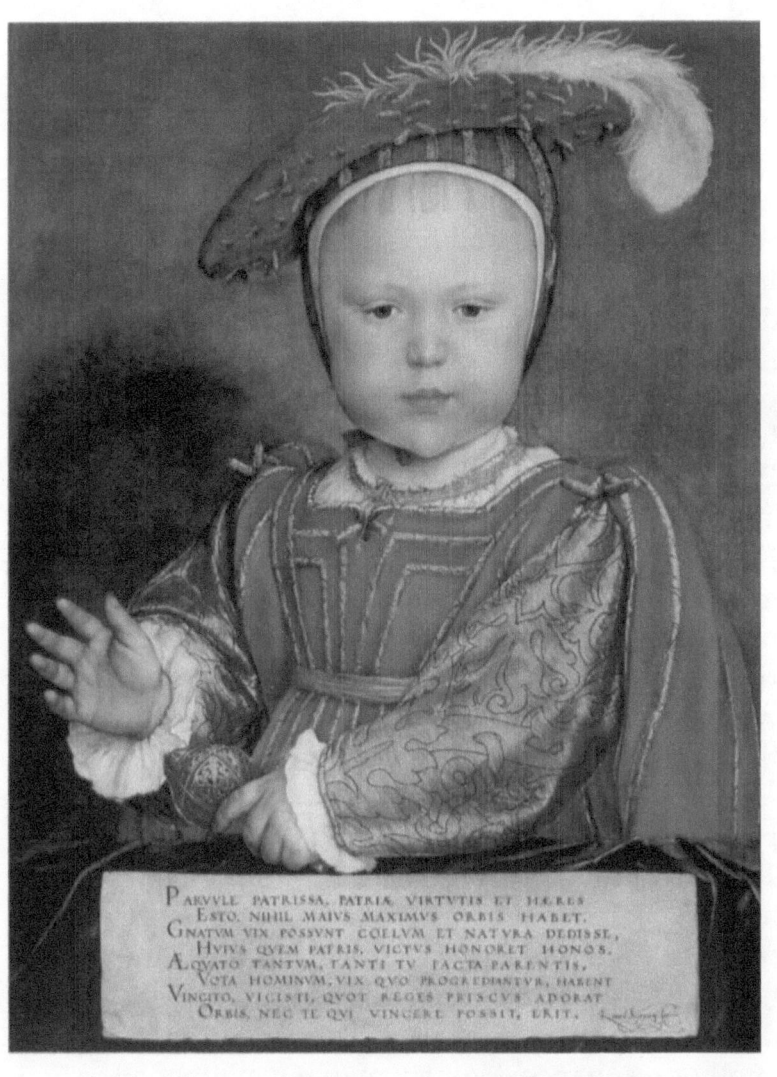

Portrait of Edward VI as a child, c.1538
Oil on panel

Edward VI (1537-1553), king of England and Ireland from 1547 to 1553, was King Henry VIII's only legitimate son; his mother, Henry's third wife, Jane Seymour, died 12 days after his birth. Although Edward has traditionally been viewed as a frail child who was never in good health, some recent authorities have maintained that until several years before his death he was a robust, athletically inclined youth. His tutors found him to be intellectually gifted, a precocious student of Greek, Latin, French, and theology. On Jan. 28, 1547, Henry VIII died and Edward succeeded to the throne. He died in 1553 at the age of 15.

Edward stands behind a parapet and against a monochrome background of bright blue that has turned greeny-brown over the centuries. He raises his right hand in a quasi-majestic wave to the viewer, while in his left hand he holds a priceless gold rattle that is reminiscent of a royal sceptre. The rich, lustrous red gown with gold brocaded sleeves also indicates the princely status of the child.

The baby prince looks considerably more mature than his two years would warrant and, as in the previous portrait, his pose echoes the regal authority of his father. The gesture of the hands, found in Renaissance depictions of the infant Christ blessing onlookers, has another resonance. Holbein may have intended to legitimize the English Crown's new religious role by endowing it with the forms religious art could no longer pursue in Protestant England.

Painted on oak panel, the apparently conventional design is enlivened by the shadow behind and to the left, and the rich red, brown and gold colour combination gives a mellow impression of prescient childhood. The skill in the foreshortening of the right hand's extended fingers distracts somewhat from the flat facial features - a characteristic of Holbein's royal portraiture.

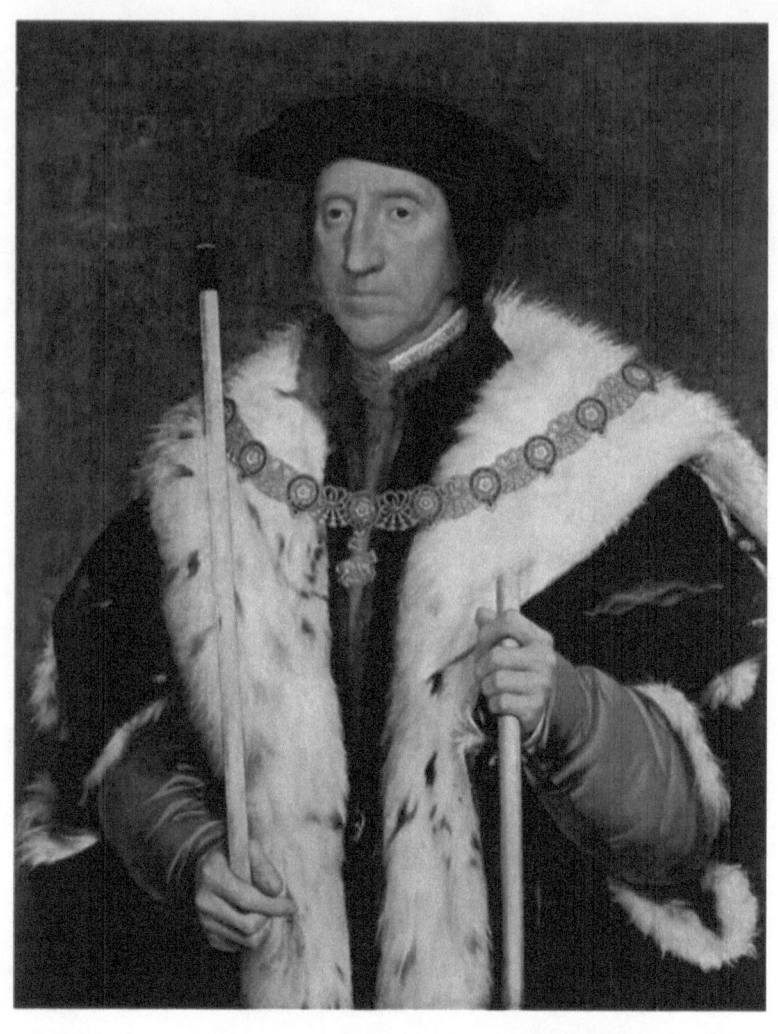

Portrait of Thomas Howard, 1539
Oil on panel

Thomas Howard (1473-1554) was a powerful English noble who held a variety of high offices under King Henry VIII. Although he was valuable to the King as a military commander, he failed in his aspiration to become the chief minister of the realm.

Howard was the brother-in-law of King Henry VII and the son of Thomas Howard, 2nd Duke of Norfolk. In May 1513 he became lord high admiral, and on September 9 he helped rout the Scots at Flodden Field near Branxton, Northumberland. He became lord deputy of Ireland in 1520 but soon left this post to command a fleet against the French.

Succeeding his father as Duke of Norfolk in 1524, he headed the faction opposed to Henry's chief minister, Thomas Wolsey. Upon Wolsey's fall in 1529, Norfolk became president of the royal council. He supported the marriage of his niece Anne Boleyn to Henry in 1533, but, by the time of Anne's fall in 1536, his relationship to Henry had already been weakened by the rise of Thomas Cromwell. As lord high steward, Norfolk was assigned to preside at her trial and execution. He momentarily regained royal favour by skillfully suppressing the rebellion of Roman Catholics in northern England known as the Pilgrimage of Grace (1536). A conservative in religion, Norfolk became a leading opponent of two influential church reformers: the king's chief adviser, Thomas Cromwell, and the archbishop of Canterbury, Thomas Cranmer. Upon Cromwell's execution (1540) Norfolk emerged as the second most powerful man in England, but his position was again weakened when Henry's fifth wife, Catherine Howard - another of Norfolk's nieces - was put to death in 1542.

In December 1546 Norfolk was accused of being an accessory to the alleged treasonable activities of his son, Henry Howard, Earl of Surrey. Surrey was executed and Norfolk condemned, but before the sentence could be carried out Henry VIII died (January 1547). Norfolk remained in prison during the reign of the Protestant king Edward VI (reigned 1547-53); in August 1553, following the accession of Queen Mary (reigned 1553-58), a Roman Catholic, he was released and restored to his dukedom. He died in 1554 after failing to suppress the uprising, led by Sir Thomas Wyat, protesting the marriage of Mary I to King Philip of Spain.

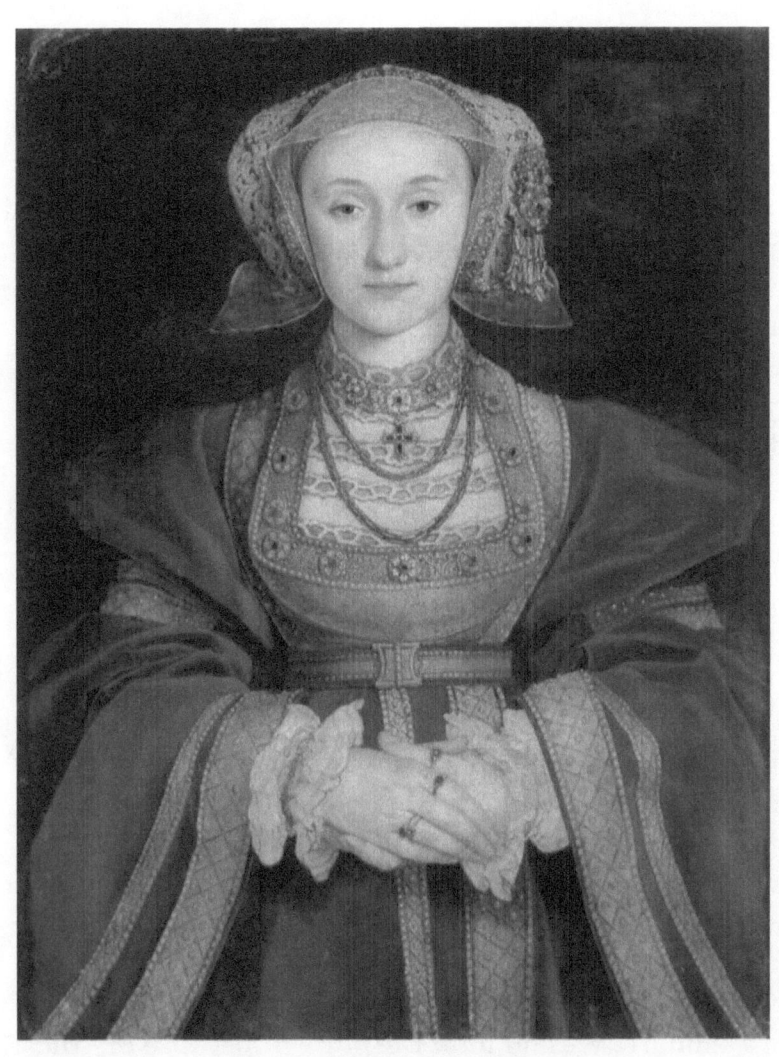

Portrait of Anne of Cleves, c. 1539
Parchment mounted on canvas

In 1539, Holbein was sent to Dьren, in the Duchy of Cleves, to paint a portrait of Anne as a possible candidate for marriage. Despite its bland, unprepossessing appearance, this royal commission is coloured by a controversial history. Holbein was placed in an impossible position: despatched to Dьren with orders to produce an instant likeness of Henry VIII's next intended bride, he needed to exercise diplomacy and tact - he would have had to show the results of his rapid sittings to the foreign officials. As it is, Anne's dress seems to have fascinated him more than the strangely lifeless symmetry of her features.

As the Paris portrait is painted on parchment and not on a difficult-to-transport wooden panel, it could have been painted on the spot, or at least well prepared by Holbein. The point of the picture was to give Henry as close an idea of the woman's appearance as possible. This would explain the frontal position, in which every detail of the face can be examined.

Henry's displeasure at finding Anne of Cleves more like a `fat flanders mare' when she arrived for the marriage ceremony in January 1540 cost Holbein dear in prestige, and he received no further important work from this quarter.

Belying her appearance, Anne of Cleves, like Christina of Denmark, was no fool. Despite - or because of - the evident humiliation of the failed marriage she obtained a handsome settlement from Henry and lived in quiet comfort in England until 1555. Henry's two subsequent wives were English.

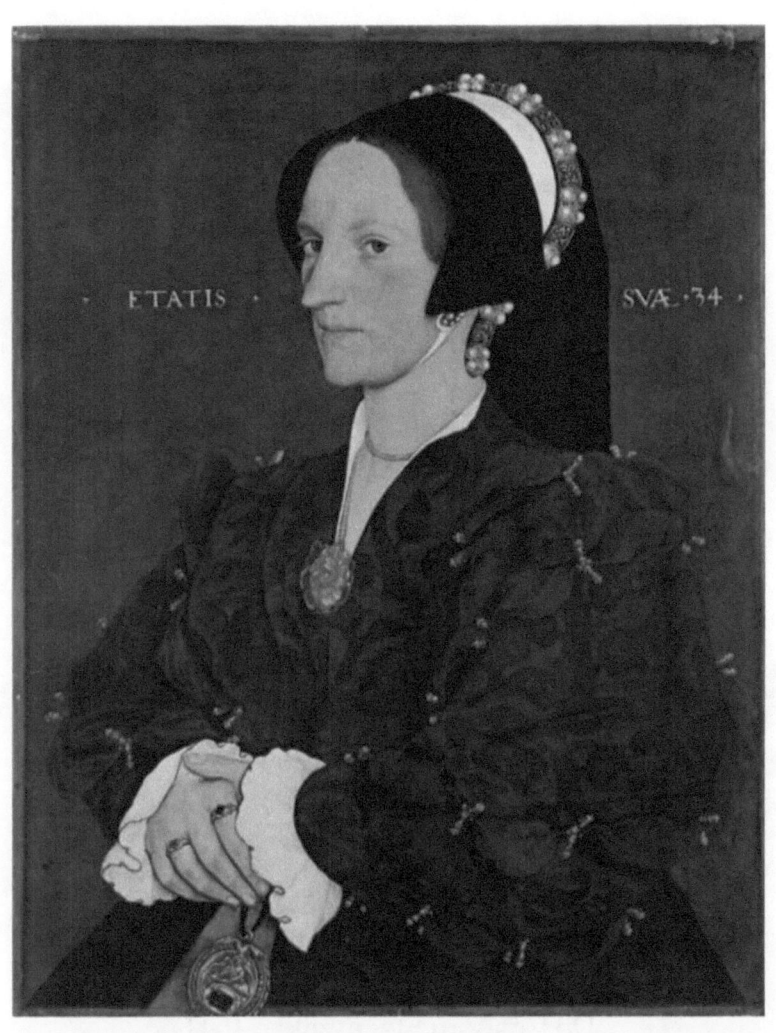

Portrait of Margaret Wyatt, Lady Lee, 1540
Oil on wood

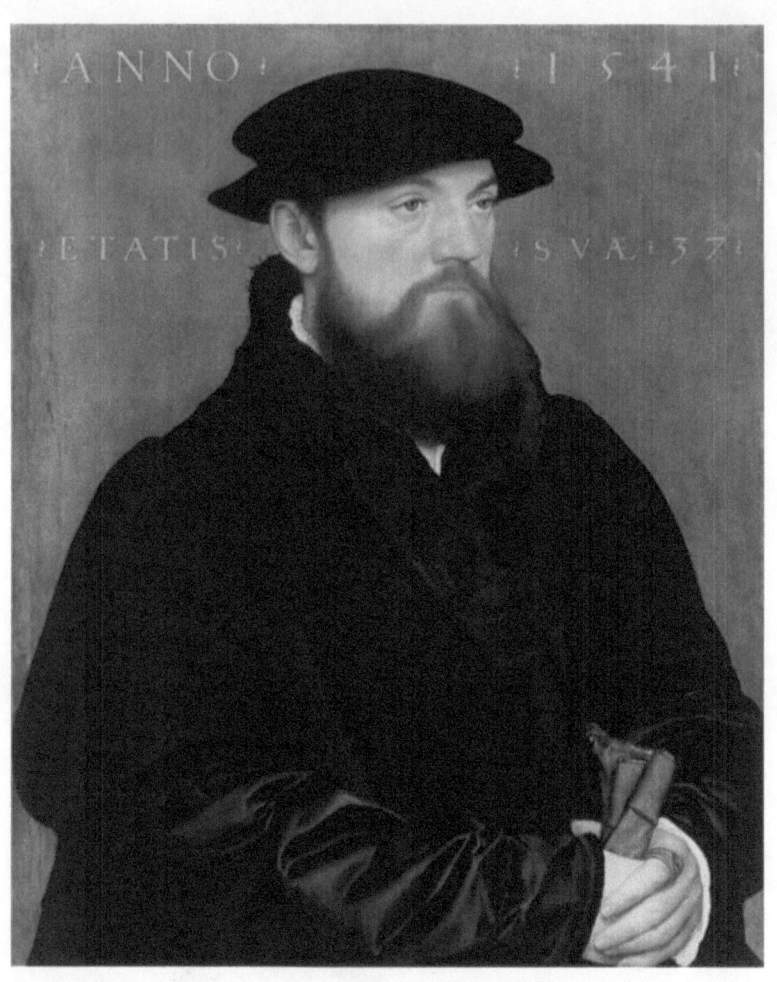

De Vos Van Steenwijk, c.1541
Oil on panel

The sitter, a member of a Dutch family, has been identified through the coat of arms inscribed on his index-finger ring. The portrait shows a considerable tightening and simplifying of the composition that would pervade Holbein's oeuvre in the last few years of his life. Rich, shiny blacks come into favour, handsomely set against the passive blue background with its gilt inscription. The articulation of light against dark grows bolder too; the faces and hands gain in emphasis and a monumental linearity emerges in the treatment of the clothing against the background. This stylistic development was perhaps a reaction against the small-scale filigree required for the portrait miniatures which were being produced in increasing numbers during this period, although both formats share the use of flat blue backgrounds.

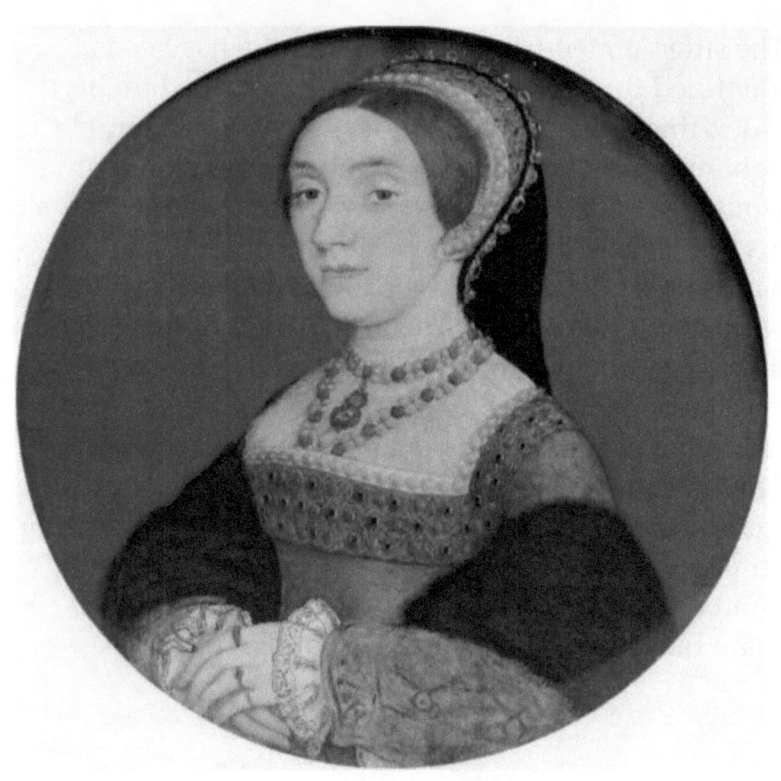

Portrait of an Unknown Lady, c.1541
Oil on panel

The first portrait miniatures were produced in France, their precursors being the small circular works commissioned by Francis I to celebrate the victory of Marignano in 1515. Jean Clouet was among the early practitioners of this format, which seems to have arrived in England by 1526 in the form of French royal portraits. Ten years elapsed before Holbein's contribution, but his work marks an immediate advance over the productions of earlier native practitioners like Lucas Horenbout. The small scale and different medium - vellum mounted on playing card (and termed `miniature' because of the lead, Latin minium, used in the paint) did nothing to hamper Holbein's sturdy realism.

The identity of the lady is uncertain - the Romantic view of the 1840s judged it to be a portrait of Henry VIII's tragic fifth wife, Catherine Howard, executed for alleged adultery, although no ascertainable portrait of her exists elsewhere. What is certain is that Holbein's powers of characterization lost nothing in the confined space. Features of his late style include the clarity and simplicity of the background, often eschewing even the standard biographical information so as to maintain as direct a perception of the sitter as possible.

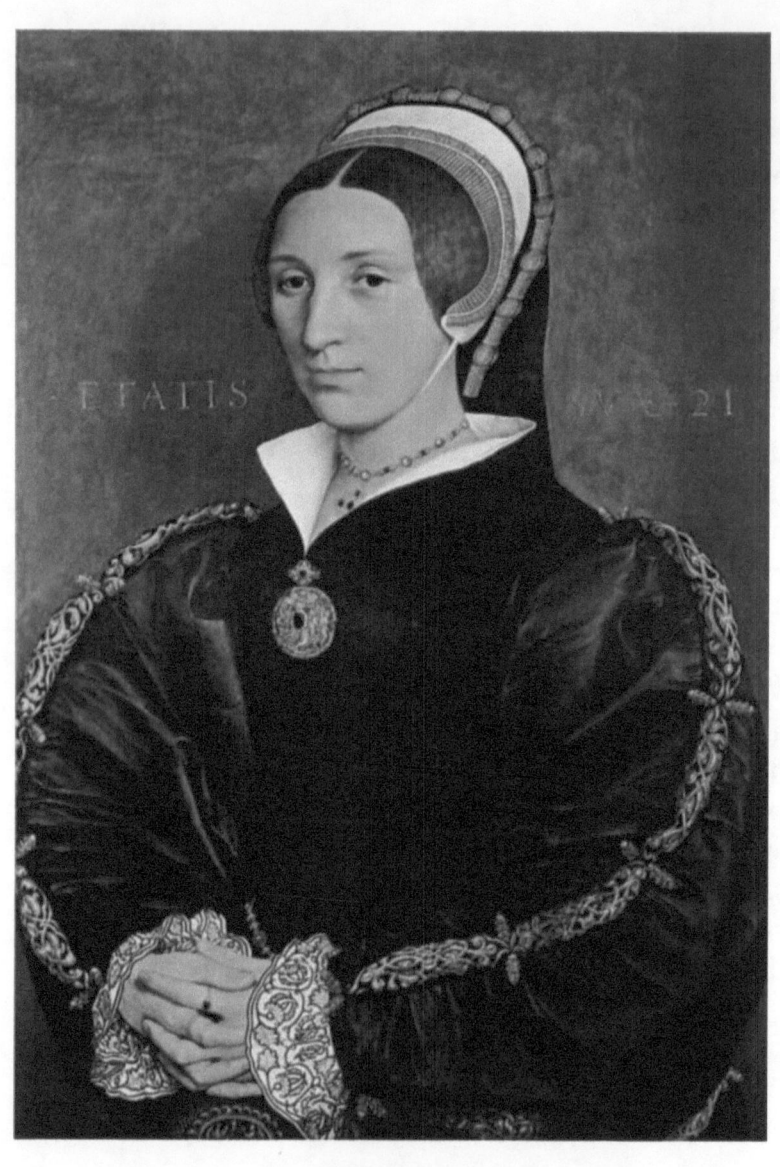

Portrait of Catarina Howard, c.1541
Oil on panel

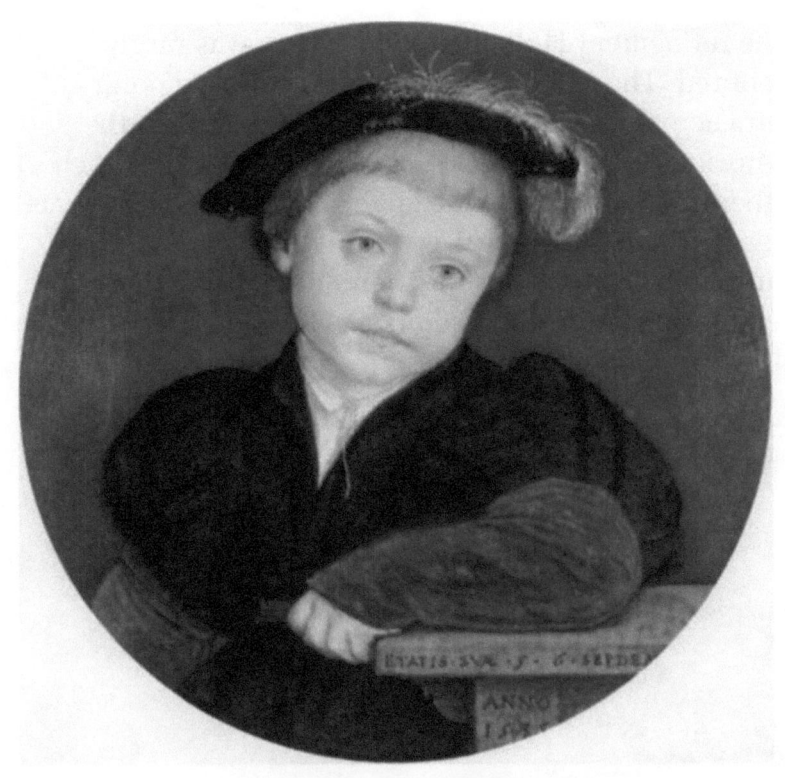

Portrait of Charles Brandon, 1541
Tempera on wood

The pair of pendant portraits of the near-royal relatives
and schoolfellows of Prince Edward (Henry Brandon
and Charles Brandon) shows that the distilled power of
quiet observation that is Holbein's main achievement in
miniature `limning' could draw personality and
character even out of the very young. Both boys appear
as differentiated individuals; Henry impatient with the
sitting, on the verge of becoming fractious, the more
stolid Charles transfixed by his role as sitter.

The refinement Holbein displays here was rarely bettered. The sad fate of the children casts a poignant aura across their portraits; the brothers died of the notorious `sweating sickness' within an hour of each other in 1551. Because the elder died first, Charles was deemed to have been (very briefly) the third Duke of Suffolk, heir to the bosom-friend of Henry VIII's youth, whose third wife had been Henry's sister, Mary, the dowager Queen of France.

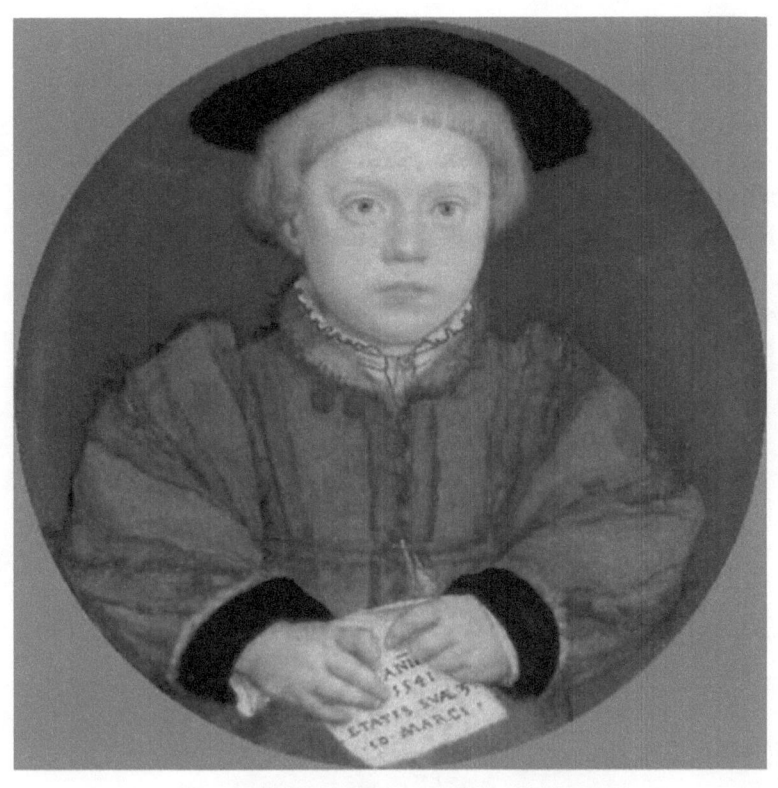

Henry Brandon, 1541
Vellum mounted on playing card
The pair of pendant portraits of the near-royal relatives
and schoolfellows of Prince Edward (Henry Brandon
and Charles Brandon) shows that the distilled power of
quiet observation that is Holbein's main achievement in
miniature `limning' could draw personality and
character even out of the very young. Both boys appear
as differentiated individuals; Henry impatient with the
sitting, on the verge of becoming fractious, the more
stolid Charles transfixed by his role as sitter.

The refinement Holbein displays here was rarely bettered. The sad fate of the children casts a poignant aura across their portraits; the brothers died of the notorious `sweating sickness' within an hour of each other in 1551. Because the elder died first, Charles was deemed to have been (very briefly) the third Duke of Suffolk, heir to the bosom-friend of Henry VIII's youth, whose third wife had been Henry's sister, Mary, the dowager Queen of France.

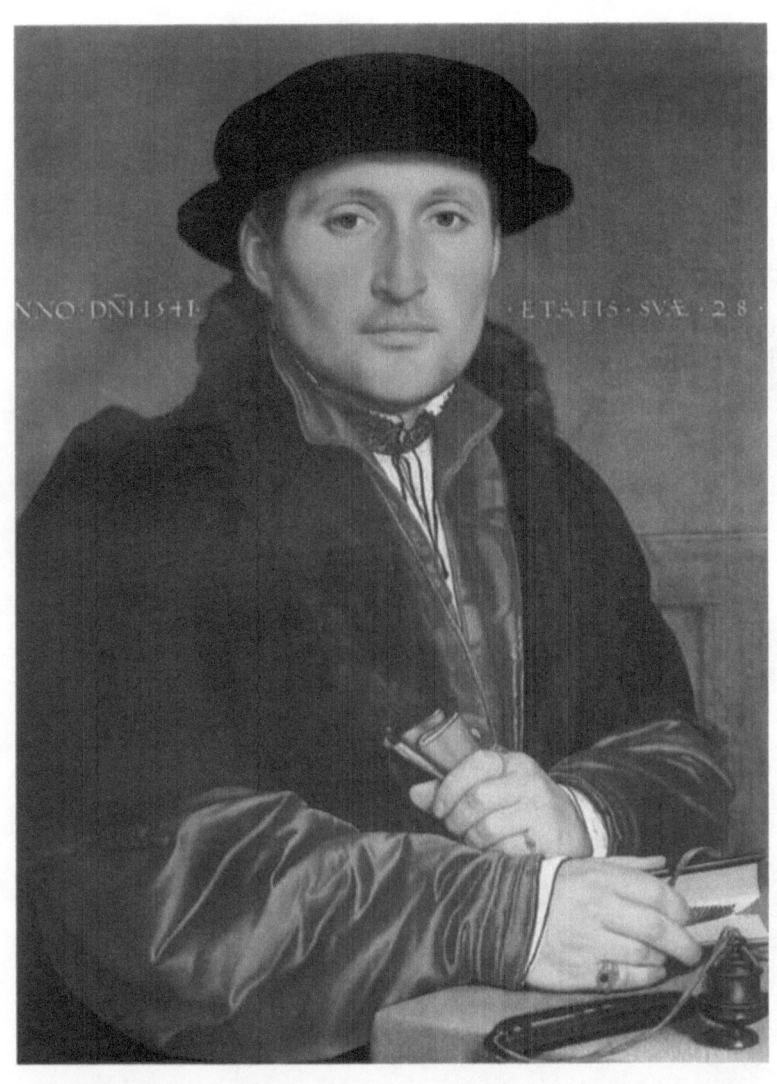

Unknown Young Man at his Office Desk, c.1541
Oil on wood

The awkwardness of the sitter's pose may result from its being an amalgam of two portraits of other people from about a decade earlier. This may explain the harder, more emphatically linear treatment of clothing and facial modelling, reminiscent of Holbein's style of the early 1530s.

The portrait has the static poise and fixity of the miniatures but on a larger scale, which allows scope for the addition of accoutrements. As in the picture of Derich Born (Royal Collection, Windsor), whose frontal gaze is so similar, the questioning directness pierces the viewer's conviction that it is merely a painted image. Although Hilliard's art would have different technical procedures, he wrote in The Arte of Limning (c.1600) of the reputation Holbein gained for the veracity of his work: `(there) came the most excelent Painter and limner Master Haunce Holbean the greatest Master Truly in both thosse arts after the liffe that ever was, so Cunning in both together and the neatest; and therewithall a good inventor, soe compleat for all three, as I never heard of any better than hee. Yet had the King in wages for limning Divers others, but Holbean's maner of limning I have ever imitated and howld it for the best...'

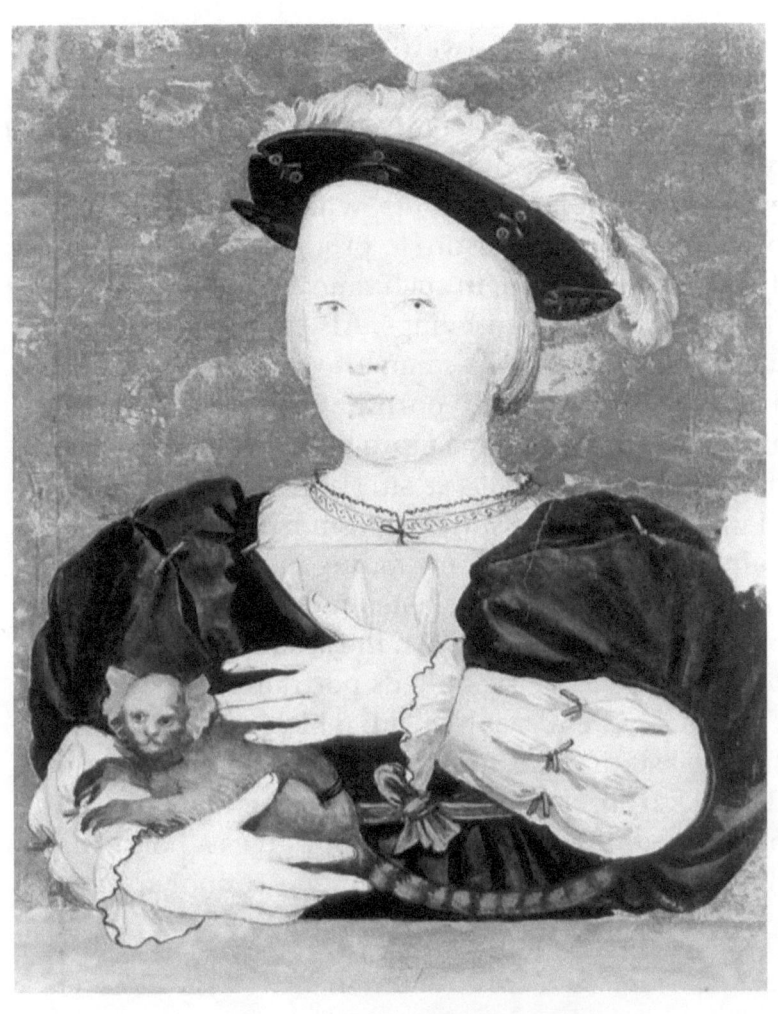

Edward, Prince of Wales, with Monkey, 1541-42
Pen, ink and watercolour

Holbein died when Edward was in his sixth year; portraits of the prince as an older boy were ascribed to Holbein until the nineteenth century, due to a mistaken reading of the date of the artist's death. This work is evidently from late in his life, when he seems to have been under great pressure to produce court portraits of a smaller dimension, in such time as could be wrested from diplomatic journeyings. Also, perhaps because few regal commissions came his way after the debacle around Anne of Cleves' portrait, he lowered his sights and produced drawings more highly coloured than those of the early 1530s as substitutes for paintings. Many of these have suffered from being hung as paintings as a result, some fading in sunlight as is the case here. Nevertheless, beneath the ghostlike outlines of the boy's face can be seen the attempt by Holbein to parallel aspects of the father's portrait in the Museo Thyssen-Bornemisza, Madrid; which goes beyond sartorial similarities to the bulky, frontal pose and the flat background, while the sketchy, spontaneous handling of the brushed-on colour gives a poignancy to the work more measured treatments cannot approach.

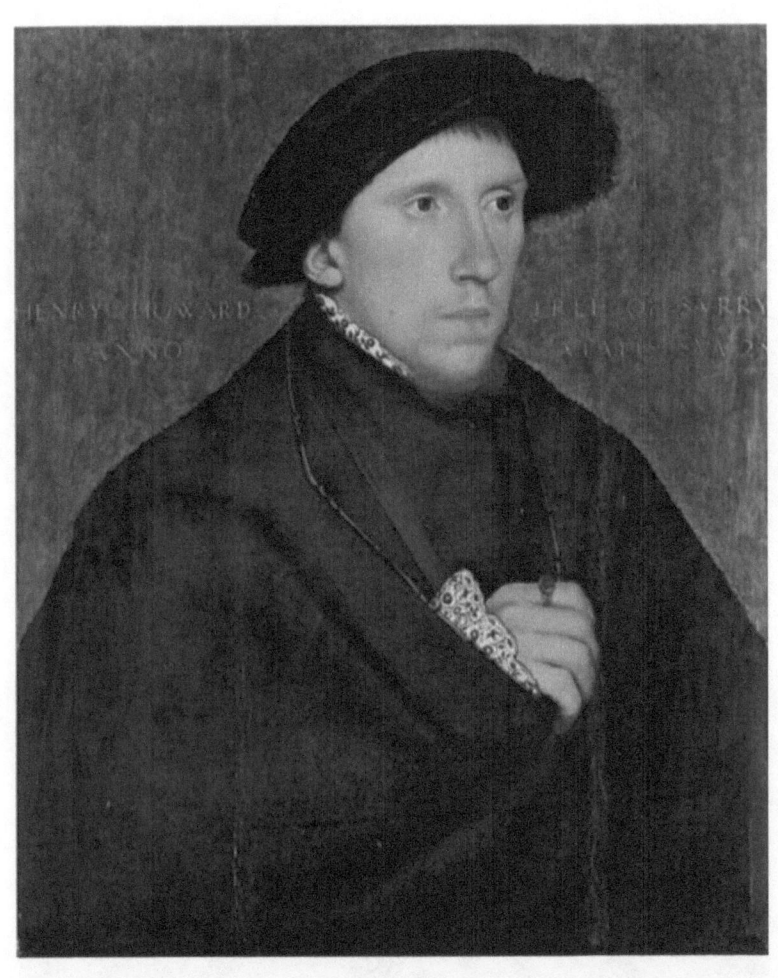

Henry Howard, Earl of Surrey, c.1542
Oil on panel
Henry Howard (1515/18-1547) was the son of Thomas
Howard, Duke of Norfolk. In December 1546 he was
accused of treasonable activities and was executed.

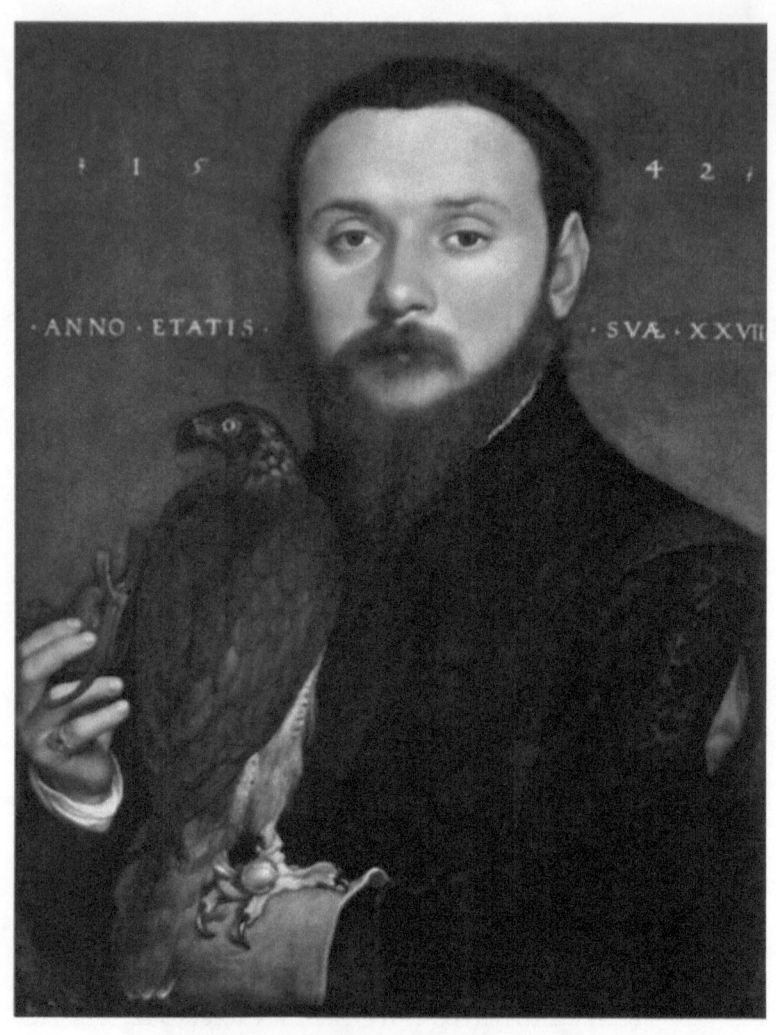

Portrait of Nobleman with a falcon, 1542
Tempera on panel

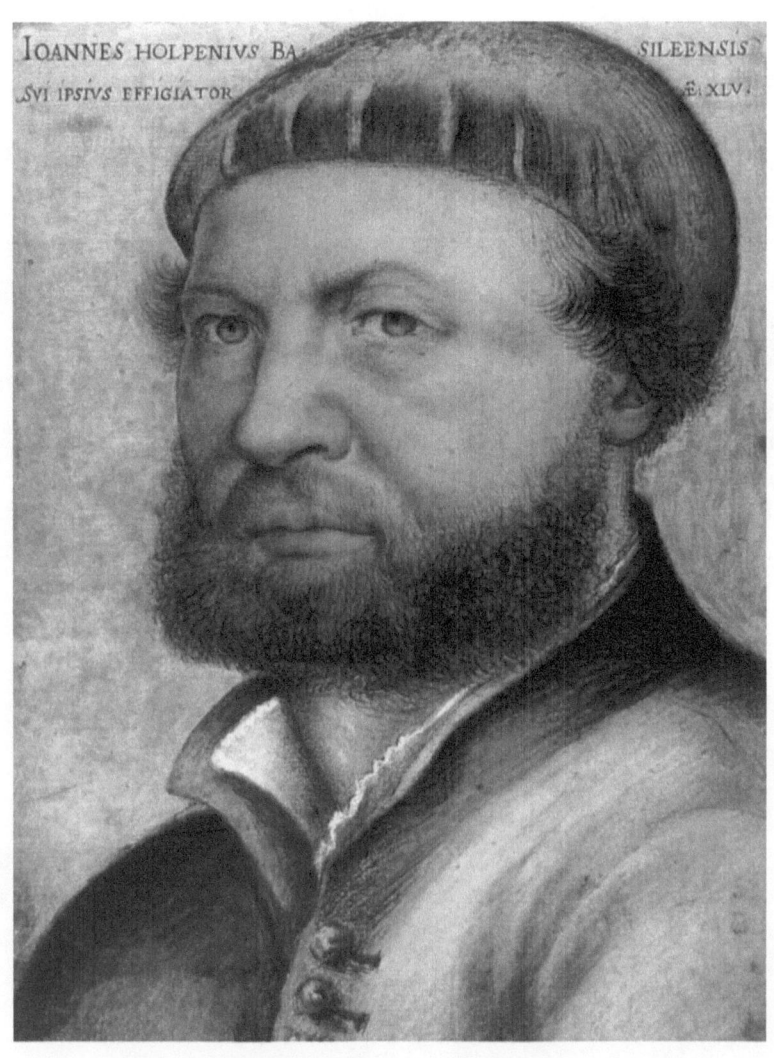

Self-Portrait, 1542-43
Coloured chalks and pen, heightened with gold

Although the gold background is of a later date, the wording of the Latin inscription at the top of the picture is presumably authentic. According to this, the picture is a self portrait of Johannes Holbein of Basel at the age of 45. The painter died not long after in London, probably of the plague. Holbein arrests the viewer with his direct gaze, which suggests he was looking into a mirror. An unusual feature is the use of blue pastel, for which there is scarcely any precedent. Thanks to the inscription, the colour-based composition and fine modeling of the face, the picture acquires the character of a painting and looks not so much like a preparatory study for a panel painting but rather like an original portrait.

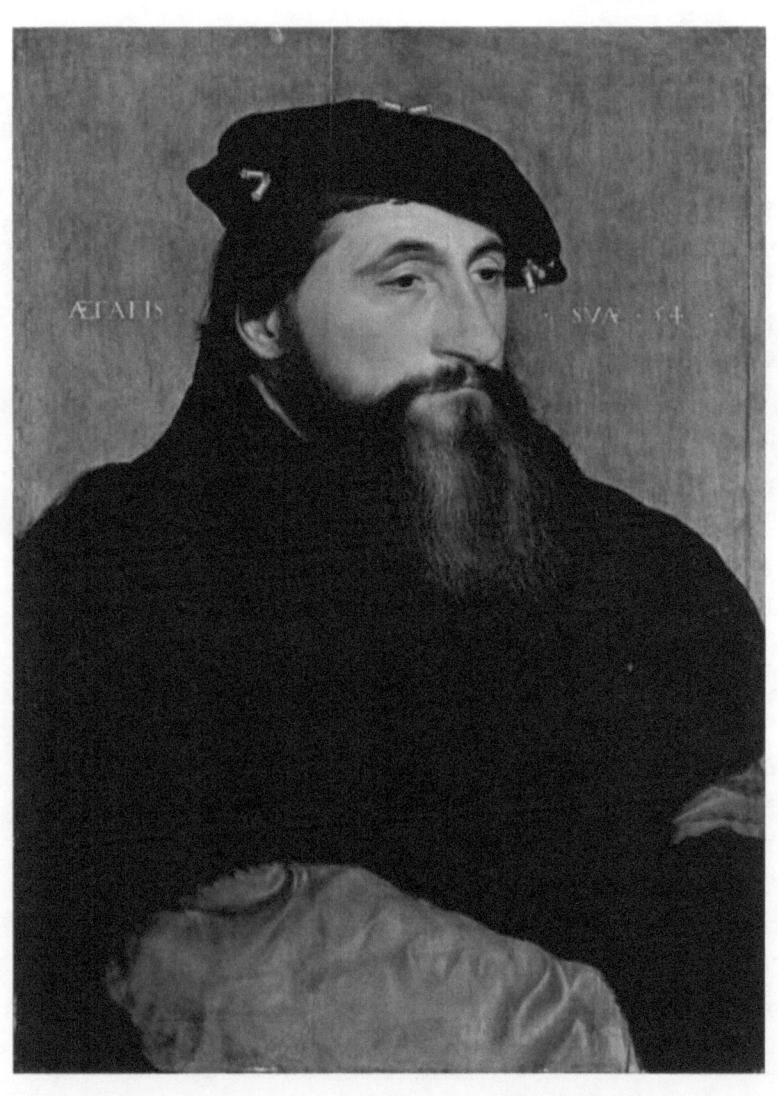

Duke Anton the Good of Lorraine, 1543
Oil on panel

The identification of the 54-year-old man is not completely certain, but it is most probably Duke Antony of Lorraine (1489-1544), who was a commander in the service of the French king, Francis I. The portrait is dated to the last year of Holbein's life on stylistic grounds. As the duke was not in England at that time, the picture could be based on a study that the painter did in 1538, when he also painted a portrait of Duke Antony's daughter, Anne.

Whoever the subject may have been, Holbein's extraordinary control over the execution and painting invests the work with an authority that not even Jean Clouet at the French court could match. The linearity of the black cape is prefigured in a number of works from the 1530s, but without the soft richness shown here. The texture of the sleeve rivals Titian's achievements. There is an absence of the sheen Holbein prefers elsewhere, as on velvet or satin. Surrounding imagery is kept to a minimum and nothing detracts from the bold monumentality of the figures. The thin gold of the inscription echoes the sprigs of gold in the cap. This refinement vanished from English painting after Holbein's death and the vigour and often splendid coloration that marks native production for the rest of the century could not encompass the truth to appearances which Holbein had made his goal.

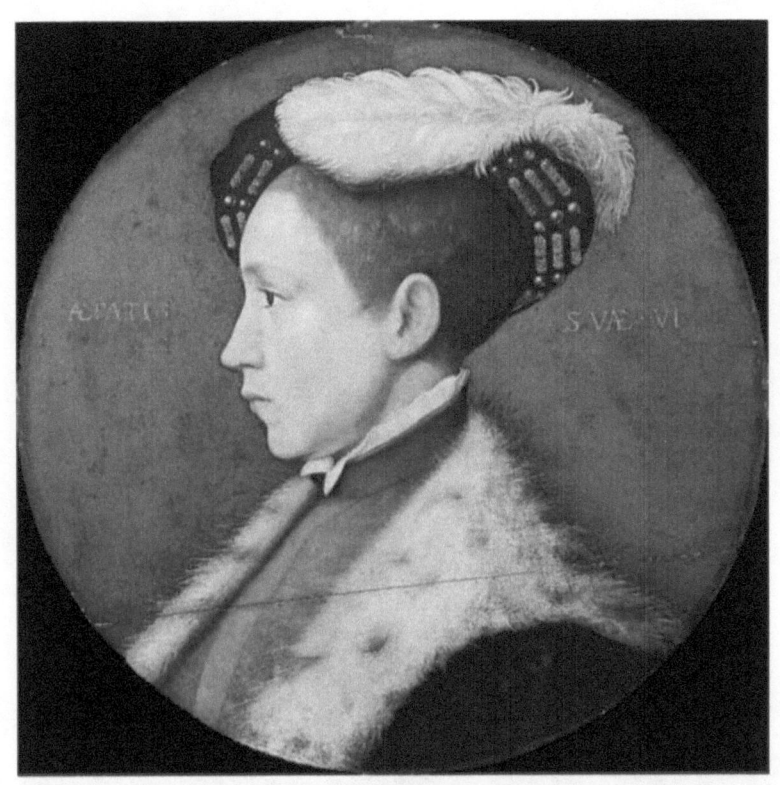

Edward, Prince of Wales, 1543
Oil on panel

The inscription on the background shows the age (6) of the sitter, the son of Henry VIII. Some scholars assume, based on X-ray investigations revealing a garment corresponding to the fashion in 1546, that the painting was executed by an imitator (William Scrots) in 1546. However, it is generally accepted as the last work of Hans Holbein.

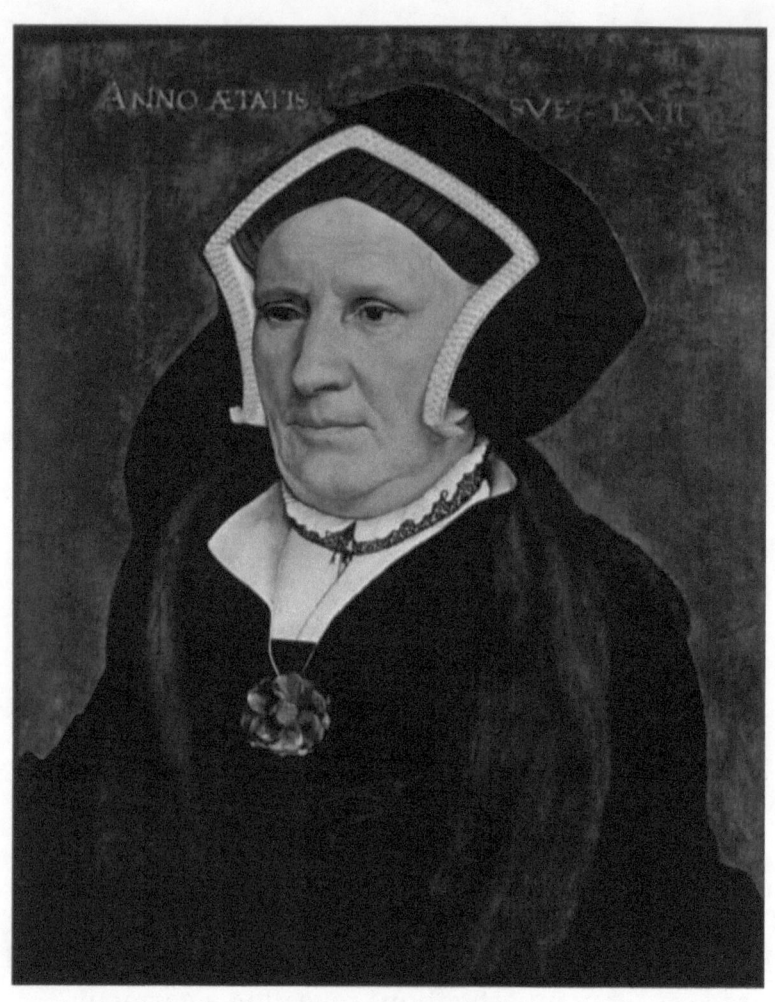

Lady Butts, c.1543
Oil on panel

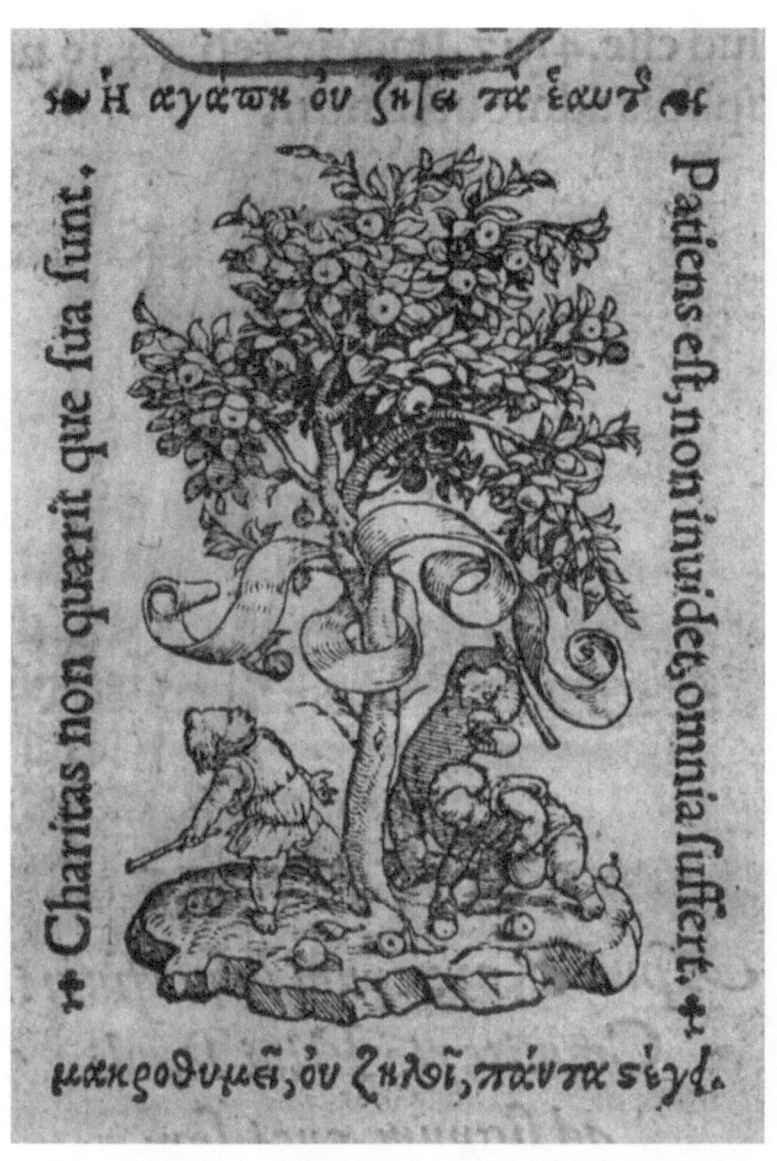

Charitas, 1543
Woodcut

In 1543 Holbein drew an inscribed CHARITAS sign for the Netherlandish Protestant book printer Reynold Wolf, who worked in London. This took the form of an apple tree whose fruits could be harvested by the 'children of God.'

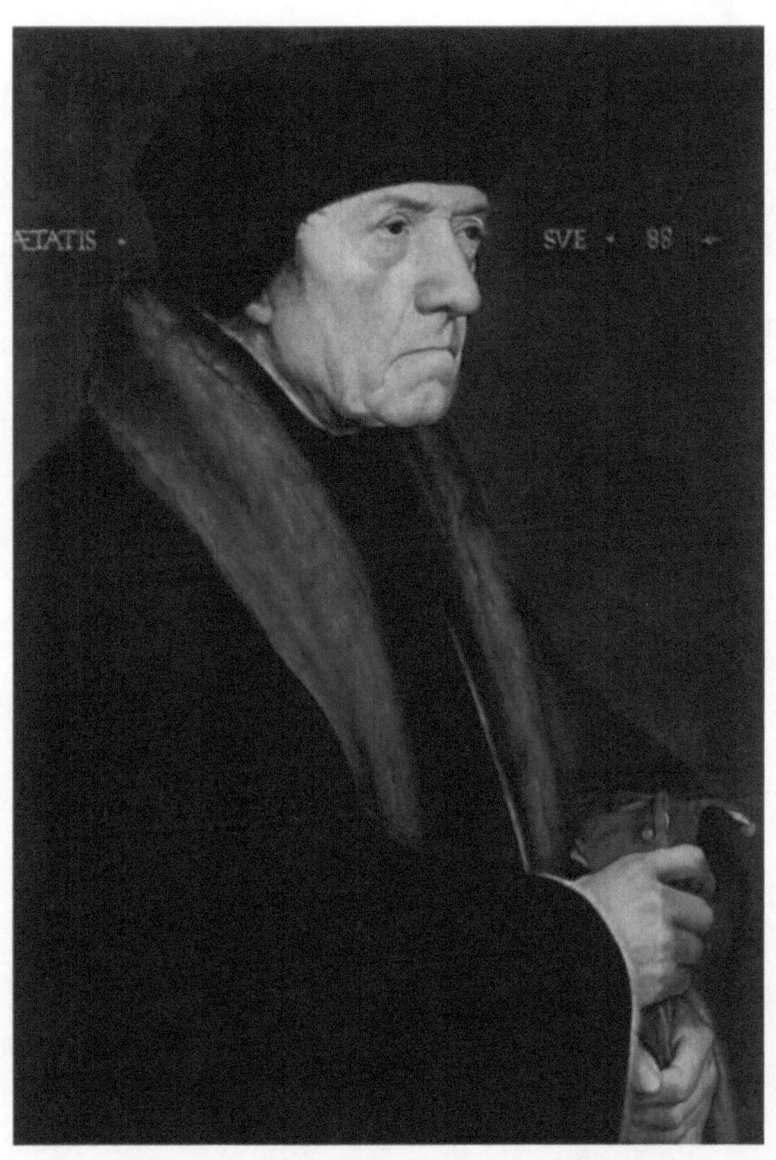

Portrait of Dr. John Chambers, c.1543
Oil on wood

John Chambers was 88 years old when Holbein executed this portrait. The close similarity of the sitter with the man identified as Chambers in the barber surgeons' picture (on Henry's right) allow a definite identification. Chambers was a cleric who also distinguished himself as a doctor. He was so successful in this profession that Henry VIII appointed him one of his personal physicians.

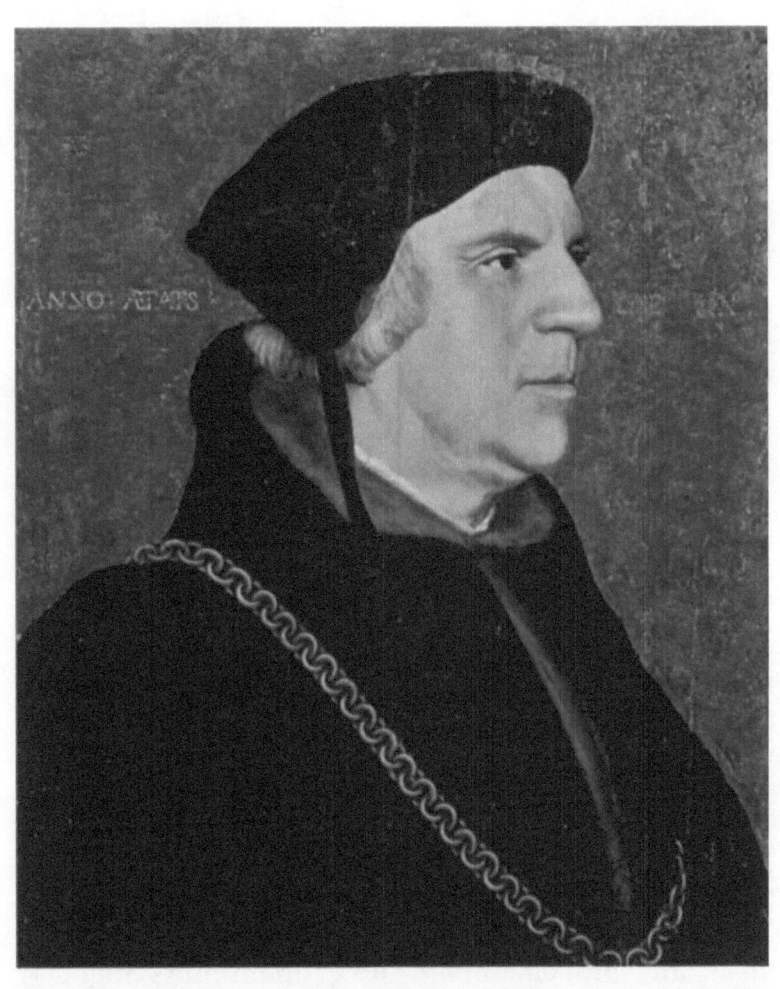

Sir William Butts, c.1543
Oil on panel
Sir William Butts, a professor at the Cambridge
University, was the physician of Henry VIII.

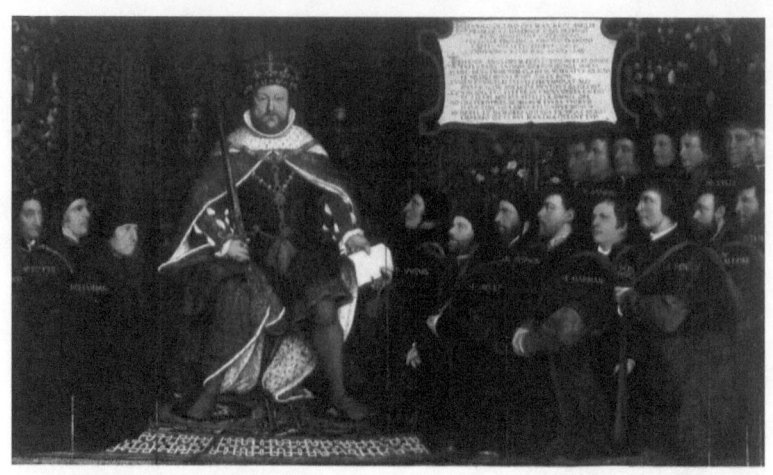

Henry VIII and the Barber Surgeons, c. 1543
Oak,

Sitting enthroned and facing the viewer directly, Henry
VIII pays no attention to the other figures in the picture.
With his left hand he holds out a sealed document that
is being taken by Thomas Vicary, the Master of the
Barber Surgeons' Company. Various other members of
the guild described by name are placed on the right
beside Vicary, some of them added later in the century.
Kneeling on the left of the picture are the two royal
physicians John Chambers and William Butts, together
with the royal apothecary Thomas Alsop, none of
whom were members of the Barber Surgeons'
Company.